Know Your Story
and Lead with It

Know Your Story and Lead with It

The Power of Narrative in Clergy Leadership

Richard L. Hester & Kelli Walker-Jones

THE
ALBAN
INSTITUTE

Herndon, Virginia
www.alban.org

The Alban Institute
2121 Cooperative Way, Suite 100
Herndon, VA 20171

Unless otherwise noted, all Scripture quotations are from the New Revised Standard Version of the Bible, © 1989, Division of Christian Education of the National Council of Churches of Christ in the United States of America, and are used by permission.

The excerpt on page 27 was first published in the article "Early Memory and Narrative Therapy" by Richard L. Hester in *The Journal of Individual Psychology* Volume 60 Issue 4, pp 339–347. Copyright © 2004 by the University of Texas Press. All right reserved. Excerpted with permission.

Cover design by Signal Hill.

Cover art: This art is a detail of a watercolor that was made by a narrative clergy peer group in the authors' Sustaining Pastoral Excellence Project. It was done as part of a one-day retreat, the purpose of which was to allow the group members unique opportunities to express themselves in unconventional ways. Using watercolor, each participant filled two pages with color. Afterward, the group collaborated in making a collage by cutting and pasting their pages into a lively composition. The simplicity of materials and childlike task evoked memories and images. The group process incorporated elements of working alone and working in cooperation, negotiating about how the different elements would be used. The joyfulness of the artwork expresses the camaraderie of the ministers whose stories are told in this book. Our thanks to Sue Etheridge, MA ATR, the art therapist who developed and led this activity.

Library of Congress Cataloging-in-Publication Data
Hester, Richard L. (Richard Loren)
  Know your story and lead with it : the power of narrative in clergy leadership / Richard L. Hester and Kelli Walker-Jones.
      p. cm.
  Includes bibliographical references.
  ISBN 978-1-56699-388-3
  1. Pastoral theology. 2. Storytelling--Religious aspects--Christianity. 3. Christian leadership. I. Walker-Jones, Kelli. II. Title.
  BV4011.3.H47 2009
  253'.7--dc22
                    2009019979

        09   10   11   12   13   VP   5   4   3   2   1

For Beverly

For Logan, Kate, and Sarah,
and for Alice

Contents

Foreword

While reading this book, I could not help but think of Richard Adams's *Watership Down*. That association may seem quite odd. After all, Richard Hester and Kelli Walker-Jones tell the story of clergy and the challenge of leadership by clergy. Adams tells a story about a few rabbits having to flee their warren when it is threatened by destruction. Yet I think there are great parallels between these books.

Adams's story of the disparate group of rabbits trying to find a new home is also a story of leadership. Hazel, a rabbit who is thrust into leadership as the rabbits undertake a hazardous journey to find a new home, is forced to discover along the way what it means to be a leader. What he learns is that to lead well he must depend on those he leads. He must learn to listen. He must learn how to acknowledge that he is not sure what they should do; and he must, nonetheless, say, "We must do this." Because he must be willing to make a decision when it is not clear what the decision should be, he invites the group to discover resources they did not know they had. So *Watership Down* becomes a wonderful example of what Hester and Walker-Jones call "higher ignorance."

Hazel's leadership, however, is shaped by the canonical stories shared by rabbits about their great prince El-ahrairah, who is the exemplification of what it means to be a rabbit. In particular, El-ahrairah must learn to live by the speed of his legs and the wit of his intelligence. When rabbits seek to make themselves safe, they lose both the power of their legs and the wit of their intelligence. So Hazel must learn to lead in a manner that cannot make those that follow him safe. We see in Hazel's leadership the exemplification of El-ahrairah's reliance on his strengths and intelligence.

In many ways, Hester and Walker-Jones's book can be read as an extended commentary on the insight of *Watership Down*. The authors help us see how leadership involves the great challenge of knowing our story in light of the gospel story. They rightly emphasize how difficult it is to discover the stories that live through us. To discover the stories we live out but fail to acknowledge is often a painful process in truth-telling. But drawing on the wisdom they have gained through experience of an enacted group process, they help us see how the discovery of stories called "gospel" can be at once liberating and empowering. I am particularly impressed by how they help us locate the role of poetry.

I am confident that this book represents an important alternative to the despair that often grips those in ministry. The ministry may be one of the loneliest tasks in our culture. Loneliness can lead to self-hatred and manipulative forms of human interaction. By creating zones of trust, Hester and Walker-Jones provide a context in which ministers are able to realize they are not alone. This happens when they are able to share the stories of both success and failure that shape their lives. In the process, ministers are able to thicken what Hester and Walker-Jones identify as the "thin narratives" that too often shape the lives of those in the ministry.

Finally, I was extraordinarily impressed by their account of the importance of what they call "muscle memory"—a way of suggesting how habits are crucial for our ability to remember stories truthfully so that we may live truthful lives. These habits include transformations of speech that invite others to lead in a way that does not disempower those who are led. For it turns out that leadership is really a form of hospitality that begins by trusting others to offer us hospitality. We are in Hester and Walker-Jones's debt for reminding us of that simple but profound reality.

Stanley Hauerwas
Gilbert T. Rowe Professor of Theological Ethics
Duke University

Acknowledgments

As we look back over our six years of this project—a work that finally led to the publication of this book—we are astonished by the number of people who contributed to it. First, we thank the twenty clergy who took part in the project and who must remain anonymous. They told us their stories—intimate stories of their life and work. They collaborated with us to develop a narrative understanding of clergy leadership. In so many ways they are the authors of this book.

Suzanne Ware Luper, director of the Triangle Pastoral Counseling Center in Raleigh, North Carolina, and the staff and board of the Center, agreed to host our project. They approved our seeking two grants from Lilly Endowment Inc. to fund this Sustaining Pastoral Excellence Project. And they continued to support and encourage us during the six years of the project.

Suzanne, Barbara Mann, and David Verner joined Kelli and Dick to make up the project staff. Mahan Siler and Eunice Holbert each served terms as our staff consultant. They chaired staff meetings and met monthly with Kelli and Dick. Jennifer Clarke Brown served as research assistant, helping us assemble the data on which the book is based. Doreen Bouchard handled the many details of hospitality and financial management for the project.

An advisory board of people from the community joined the project as a part of the second grant. This board helped us think through what it would take to sustain the project beyond the limits of grant money. And they helped us translate narrative ideas into language that persons who had no prior acquaintance with narrative thought could understand. Board members were Steve Smith (chair), Janice Virtue, Janice Odom, and Henry Mitchell. At the request of the Advisory Board, two ministers from the project were added to the Board.

Two people introduced the power of art to shape personal and group identity. Logan Jones facilitated a workshop on poetic analysis and showed us how anyone can write poetry. Sue Etheridge taught us the power of collective artwork to discern leadership patterns and build team identity. The results of this collective art grace our office walls.

This experiment with clergy could not have been undertaken without grants from the Lilly Endowment. These two grants provided resources for us to have a long-term engagement with clergy—enough time to witness them clarify their personal story, build friendships, learn a narrative way, and begin to practice narrative leadership. In the course of the project John Wimmer, our project manager at the Endowment, became a mentor who both challenged and supported us. Craig Dykstra, senior vice president for religion at the Endowment, valued our "developing intellectual capital" with a small group of clergy. We were gratified to find that Lilly did not demand success in all we set out to do. Rather, they wanted us to analyze our failures and report what we learned from them. This attitude is reflected in a sign posted near the entrance to our office with a quote by Albert Einstein: "If we knew what we were doing it wouldn't be called research."

We asked fourteen people to write letters of endorsement to the Endowment to support our initial grant. They took the risk to believe in this venture, trusting that we did know what we were doing. We are grateful that they stood up for us when we needed their advocacy.

We owe special thanks to Murphy Evans, who contributed a substantial grant to support our initial project efforts.

Finally, our list of people to recognize and thank is incomplete without naming Ulrike Guthrie, our editor. She validated our early manuscript drafts and did an artful job of editing our work. More than that, she was a mentor for us as first-time authors. "Uli" guided us to the Alban Institute and their editor Richard Bass, both of whom led us through the final steps toward a completed manuscript.

There's Always More than One Story

As co-authors, ours is an unlikely partnership. Kelli is a minister and devoted mother. Dick is a therapist and former professor. Her perspective is that of a minister relating to parishioners. His is that of a professor relating to students. She was born the year he finished high school. He and his wife, Beverly, have two adult married children and four grandchildren. She and her husband, Logan, are rearing two daughters. Kelli is an extrovert and works through problems by talking; she "hates" writing. Dick is an introvert and works out problems by writing—using an academic style shaped in twenty-one years of seminary teaching. Her writing style is free-flowing and informal; when she does write, she easily catches the reader's eye. She thrives on making and nurturing relationships and spends time on the phone doing so. For him the phone is an annoying interruption. He could survive easily on a dose of one or two calls a day. She's a feminist. He enjoys white male privileges of which he's unaware—until she points them out to him.

We Live in Story

We understand ourselves and our world by means of story. Our personal or self story holds together the past, present, and future. Our memories come to us in stories. And in the present moment we extend that story. That unfolding story of past and present takes us into the future.

At the micro level, this is how it works: At this moment Dick is working on the manuscript of the book, but he's not just thinking of the present sentence. He puts it in his story of the project and the narrative of how he and Kelli are interacting in the process. He looks at the clock and thinks, "Twenty minutes until that meeting at eleven. Do I leave this and go to the meeting? I should. But no, they can meet without me. I'm going to stay and continue this page and the next." Many stories intersect in the moment, and he has to decide how to weave them together and which story will get his primary attention. His story includes the future in the form of the overall plot of getting the book published. That story tells him where he is now in the process and the sequence he and Kelli will follow in the weeks ahead. Of course this is only one strand of the many narratives that make up his ongoing self story.

Kelli is working on the manuscript. She is distracted by the sound of swords clashing and feet hitting the wooden gym floor. The sound of children fencing reminds her to look up and check on her daughter as she takes her boxing lesson. Kelli has been looking for the e-mail that contains a section she wants to include in the book. She's saying to herself, "Where did I put that e-mail copy?" thereby moving the narrative reel backward to locate it. Surrounded by the sounds of bodies and voices, Kelli has to do her writing today at the gym. She's there because this gym doesn't look like a place to leave a sixteen-year-old girl alone. She fits this narrative into the story of her week and looks ahead to Friday, when this part of the book goes to the editor.

We understand ourselves in the form of a story, and we perceive events in the form of a narrative. Story is our access to reality. And any situation can be understood through more than one story, because no single account can tell everything that happened. This means that whatever narrative we have about something is our particular take on it. Yet our take isn't just our own; it is shaped by powerful family and cultural narratives. From the paragraphs above you can see the differences in Dick's and Kelli's self stories as they work on the task of writing the book. Her story is set in her family, and she works amid the noise of a gym. His story is all about the book, and he works in the solitude of his office.

Because we are committed to this narrative perspective, the two of us are able to accept our viewpoints not as reality itself but as our stories of reality. This keeps us out of contests of "I'm right. You're wrong."

Our aim in this book is to show ministers how to explore their story of reality, how to tell it to other group members, and to consider how it can be used as a resource for leadership. This narrative perspective holds that because there's always more than one story about a situation, we have choices about which story we will embrace.

Our book is based on our experience with groups of clergy we led over a period of more than six years. Their stories woven together create the fabric that is the backdrop of our story of narrative clergy leadership. At times in this book we refer to our work with these clergy as "the project"; it was part of a six-year Sustaining Pastoral Excellence project supported by grants from the Lilly Endowment.

The Power of Not Knowing

Many people and groups try to impose their narratives on ministers. The constant pressure to live into the preferred stories of others can be disorienting. "What's my story, and how can I be faithful to it?" is an important question for clergy to ask and to ask often.

Ben moved from a large, growing church to another large church that was in decline. Upon his arrival he was approached by Vernon, who saw himself, in Ben's words, "as the resident expert on the church," working behind the scenes to make things go his way. Vernon asked Ben, "What's your plan for the congregation?" Ben replied, "I don't have a plan," which startled Vernon and bothered him. Vernon's question tried to draw Ben into a narrative that said successful pastors know how to lead any congregation toward success. They bring a vision to the new situation that will take the congregation where it needs to go. Ben saw that Vernon wanted to know Ben's plan so he could use it to increase his own control of congregational affairs. "What are you going to do?" Vernon asked. Ben said, "I'm going to listen to the congregation. I don't know enough to have a plan."

Ben's approach didn't fit the conventional wisdom about leadership because he took a not-knowing position of curiosity instead of a knowing position of top-down direction.

During his twenty-one years of teaching seminarians, Dick moved from a knowing toward a not-knowing position. At the beginning of his teaching career he was intent on transferring knowledge from teacher to student. Over time he realized that his job was not to transfer knowledge but rather to create conditions for students to acquire knowledge and wisdom for themselves.

In the early 1990s Dick was introduced to narrative therapy. This practice challenged him even more to take a not-knowing position and to learn how to ask curious questions. Dick's desire to deepen this narrative practice led him to offer a narrative therapy seminar, now in its twelfth year, to other counselors as a way of learning more about this new theory.[1]

As he deepened his practice of narrative therapy, he also witnessed the transformative social power that not-knowing could have on an organization. The counseling center with which he is associated adopted the narrative methods, along with feminist theory, to reshape their organizational structure. This organic development drew him to wonder how a narrative approach might be useful to clergy.

Working with clergy drew Dick to a deeper level of not-knowing. In clergy groups he had neither the power of a professor nor the power of a therapist. Moreover, Kelli and the clergy groups helped him discover he did not understand the work of clergy as well as he had assumed. Divested of these powers and assumed knowledge, he truly was in a not-knowing position.

Dick says, "Most of my career was in teaching, counseling, and a stint as executive director of a counseling center. These jobs carried with them a position of institutional power. My experience with narrative clergy groups and co-leading them with Kelli introduced me to a new kind of leadership power—leading from a not-knowing position."

Kelli came to a not-knowing position by several routes. When she entered the ordained ministry, she was appointed to two small United Methodist churches in west Tennessee. She was the first woman minister to lead these churches. She had never experienced a woman as her own minister; she didn't have a role model. Kelli and the congregations became partners in not-knowing as they journeyed in faith together.

When Kelli joined this project she was a veteran coach for Odyssey of the Mind for fourth and fifth graders. Odyssey of the Mind is a creative problem-solving program. The children are given a complex project to complete. For one project they were told: Build a vehicle that can blend into three environments. The vehicle must be propelled by a person, and his/her feet cannot touch the ground. The rules say adult coaches cannot direct the project. It belongs to the children. Coaches may ask questions, teach skills, and hold boundaries, but they may not tell the children how to solve the problem. Most children love this, but the adults, both coaches and parents, have tremendous difficulty staying out of the process. They want to fix, to direct, to be the expert. Kelli had to coach her group's parents on how to ask curious, not-knowing questions.

Kelli says, "I loved the Odyssey process even though it could be chaotic. It was freeing not to be wedded to the outcome. It was jaw-dropping to witness what these elementary-aged children could imagine and do when they were given an opportunity to work with coaches who supported them and didn't tell them what to do. In the present project I saw how this not-knowing principle was as difficult for clergy—and for us as leaders—as it was for the parents in Odyssey of the Mind. Then I saw how our participants began to take a not-knowing position that opened up and deepened narratives rather than shutting them down with solutions. It has been fun to come full circle from my first experience in ministry to watching clergy participants discover the power of the not-knowing process."

What Is Narrative Leadership?

In the research for this book we also moved from a knowing to a not-knowing stance. We thought we would achieve one particular goal—that by forming clergy peer groups we would be helping pastors break out of their isolation—but we discovered that this also helped them develop a narrative way of leading. This way of leading goes against cultural expectations that say effective leaders are knowers—taking charge because they always know what to do, as Vernon expected of Ben in the story above. We came to understand that what effective clergy leaders know is their own story—and that they lead from it. This orientation makes them curious about the stories of congregations, individuals, and families. This book is about what we learned with and from clergy about narrative leadership.

Clergy have one of the most complex and daunting leadership roles of any professional. They are answerable to a whole congregation of people who have divergent views about what the leader ought to be doing. Their days are unpredictable because so many people have direct access to them. They lead a volunteer organization in which lay leaders flow in and out—constantly threatening organizational stability. Clergy leadership is an acid test for any leadership approach. If narrative leadership works here, it can surely work in other settings.

Narrative leadership promotes a different kind of social power. This power grows out of appreciation for people's stories and the often unrecognized resources that reside in those stories. When leaders invite the telling of those stories, they are helping release social power, and in this atmosphere leadership can easily be moved from one person to another. No single person possesses the leadership. All share it.

From a Programmatic to an Organic Strategy

The account of Ben and Vernon above shows the contrast between a programmatic strategy (Vernon's story) and an organic strategy

(Ben's story). Ben was intent on learning what was already going on in the congregation—its organic evolution—so he could join that narrative.

Our narrative orientation led us to take a not-knowing position toward the groups and individuals in the project. This drew us into an organic strategy. Rather than viewing the project as movement toward a pre-determined destination, we came to understand it as a pilgrimage where the focus was more on the journey than on the destination. We hope that our book will encourage you to think of your own leadership in that way.

Where to Next?

This book is an account of our pilgrimage. Each chapter tells part of the story and the narrative understanding that emerged from the journey. The book is inspired, energized, and sustained by the stories of the participants in our clergy groups. Without their stories there would be no book. Their names and the names of their congregations have been changed to protect their privacy.

The first chapter develops further the idea that "Story Is How We Think about Ourselves." Chapter two, "How Can You Know Your Story?" describes our use of different strategies to help participants explore and tell their personal or self stories. Chapter three, "Narrative Leadership," tells how clergy can lead from a narrative orientation and how "not-knowing" can be a key ingredient for effective leadership. Chapter four, "Signs of Transformation," identifies six indicators or clues that narrative work was leading participants toward some kind of transformation. Chapter five, "Leading the Congregation with Your Story," is a report of our survey of participants in 2008 to find out how they were continuing to use narrative practices. Chapter six, "Forming and Leading Narrative Clergy Peer Groups," provides practical guidance for ministers who want to organize such a group. The final section of the book provides resources for narrative clergy groups.

We hope that as you read the book you will have a sense that this is your pilgrimage, too, and we hope that our account will encourage you into narrative ventures of your own.

CHAPTER 1

Story Is How We Think about Ourselves

"It was a beautiful sunny day, perfect weather to walk to the Chinese restaurant," Kelli reported.

Peking Garden was less than a mile away, and there were sidewalks all the way. Our new clergy peer group of nine, along with Dick and me, set out to enjoy the day and the walk. I looked up when I heard a loud noise. Kathy was banging on the hood of a car and yelling for the driver to stop. A slow-moving car, driven by a distracted young woman, hadn't seen Alice from our group and had knocked her down and into the street. In seconds, everyone jumped to action. Kathy made sure the car stopped. I stepped into the street to direct traffic around Kathy, the car, and Alice, who was prone in the road. Someone called the police. Ed, a member of the group who was well-versed in first aid, knelt down to see if Alice was injured. Before long, Will spelled me as traffic director, and I went to account for the entire group.

Within a short time the emergency was addressed. Alice was all right and ended up comforting the young woman who had bumped her into the street. We continued on our way to lunch.

As we gathered for the afternoon session, the energy in the room told us that our planned agenda needed to be set aside to make room for this story. The newly formed group had just lived through a crisis and needed to debrief. When we invited everyone to tell their story about what happened, we found we had a study in story. No two stories were the same. What really happened came in eleven different versions.

As group members recounted their roles in the story and what they saw, we got a lesson in how we access reality. Everyone had a different angle. No one person had the entire truth. The accident became a springboard for the group to explore how we grasp reality through story and how our story isn't the only one.

What Is a Story?

A story is a spoken or written account of connected events. These connected events create a plot—a thread of unfolding happenings starting with an intention to head somewhere, followed by a phase of uncertainty, unpredictability, or crisis, and, finally, ending in a resolution. You can see this sequence in the story above. The plot leads hearers to ask, "What happened next?" The plot occurs within the teller's sense of "this is the way the world is." The teller has gathered pieces of information and organized them into a plot that fits her world view. The plot is moved forward by human—or humanlike—characters. The more detailed the plot, the more the personality of the characters is revealed.

Other elements shape a story; two of these are context and purpose. The *context* is the circumstance that prompts one to tell the story. In the story of Alice, the context was the collective experience of the accident. The *purpose* is the reason the storyteller tells it. The purpose for telling this story was to help the group talk about and emotionally assimilate a disturbing event. Two other purposes came into view as the stories unfolded. The telling helped knit together the relationships in this new group. It also helped the group see that "there's always more than one story."

When we tell a story of an event or series of events, we are selective. We choose only parts of an event for the plot, for we cannot possibly round up every detail of what occurred. Out of all the things that took place in the accident event, each person could collect and tell only a fraction of the total. When each one of us assembled the information for the story, we created our own version of what happened. Each version was different because each person was collecting and arranging different bits of information. As group members crafted their stories of the accident, these stories were shaped by other ongoing personal narratives. So, for example, when Will stepped into the street to direct traffic, he wondered whether any members of his congregation would pass by. What would go through their minds? In a way the congregation joined him in the street, and their presence shaped Will's version of the accident.

We select, reject, connect, pare, smooth out, lengthen this, compress that, and tidy up a messy conglomeration of information to create a story of what happened—with this car accident or any other event in our lives. And most of the information about the event lies about us on the cutting room floor. We walk off with our story, leave the remains on the floor, and go on our way. We seldom notice we've left so much behind. In this situation, however, we had the chance to hear ten other people's accounts and to see that they had gathered pieces of information we hadn't noticed and had created a film somewhat different from ours.

This gap between what actually took place and what people can tell of it is the space where a narrative approach does its primary work. Much like a movie editor trying to find essential pieces of film for a scene, a curious person can go to that heap of neglected information on the cutting room floor and find other narratives—stories that may reinforce or challenge the one that's been told. In our work with clergy, we've found that material from the cutting room floor often provides a story about the minister's strength, courage, and resourcefulness that isn't in the version being told.

Ben, from whom we've already heard, told his clergy group about two women in his community who were preparing Meals on Wheels in their church kitchen. They were attacked and stabbed by a young African American man. Later one of the women died. The city was already a tinderbox of racial tension. African American and white ministers in the community responded by organizing a series of interracial evening services. Ben said that an idea emerged for a love feast service to express the unity of the faith community and its commitment to put an end to violence. When Ben told this story, members of his clergy peer group began to ask: Who came up with the idea of the love feast? It was Ben. Who organized that service? Ben did. Who was exercising ongoing community leadership? Ben was. His peers went to the cutting room floor and retrieved information that *he* in turn had left out of this story. It went against his nature to claim these things; however, the group encouraged him to accept and appreciate these neglected parts of his vital leadership role.

The eliciting of missing details from Ben's story by listeners is a case of *thickening a thin narrative*. His first telling of the story was a thin account that omitted his personal role in the clergy group's response to the tragedy. His clergy peers weren't satisfied to accept the thin version. They took a curious, not-knowing stance toward Ben's account. That is a central idea in narrative theory: Approach stories with curiosity and don't assume you know the situation. Stay on the curious side of things. You never know what you will uncover in the heap of information that's been left on the floor.

> ### THICK AND THIN NARRATIVES
>
> Thin narratives provide a minimum of detail. "The sermon today was about grace and works. I didn't like it." That's a thin version, stripped bare of all detail and conveying almost nothing about the event or why the listener didn't like it. A thicker version: "In today's sermon Reverend Davis wrestled with the difference between what we say we believe about grace—God loving us unconditionally—and the way most of us actually live. We live like God expects us to be dutiful slaves, workaholics who can never let up. I didn't like it because it's my story, and I didn't want to hear it. I can't shake it off. But do I really want to?" This account gives detail about the message and the listener's reaction to it. His response is conflicted and leaves us wanting to know more. The thin story papers over any ambiguity or conflict and is so flat it leaves us saying, "So what?"

The Stories We Are

We think of ourselves in the form of an unfolding story. When we want to recover something from the past, we rewind the film that is our life to see the narrative there. When we think of the present, we do so in a narrative. As we're having breakfast we consider what lies ahead and what happened just a few minutes ago. Thinking about the future is done on the scaffolding of a narrative. Story holds it all together, gives it structure. All of this is an inner narrative that we couldn't possibly tell, and if we could, few would have the patience to listen to all of it. The stories we do tell, as we've seen, are culled from the narrative within us.

If we were asked to tell our inner story, that ongoing narrative about our life, most likely we'd be stumped. That story isn't something we generally think about, nor is it easy to pin down. It is so close, so intimate, so much a part of flesh and bone, that we can't see it. Yet it very much patterns how we live and what we believe about ourselves.

We are inviting you—as we did our clergy groups—to become better acquainted with your inner story. We take you back to the cutting room floor and suggest that there's a "this is my story" plot down there, and we offer ways for you to find what it is. We drew our clergy groups toward their inner story with several strategies, which we describe at length in the next chapter. Perhaps the most striking strategy is inviting them to tell us their earliest childhood memory. Alfred Adler first developed this strategy with his therapy clients. When asked to recall an early memory, Adler said, out of the incalculable number of possibilities, people select those that have a bearing on their present life situation. These early recollections are laden with clues about their "Story of My Life." Although they may not be aware of their life narrative, they are using it to understand the present and to anticipate the future with "an already tested style of action."[1]

Ed's earliest memory is at age three. He was taking a trip on the train with his father from North Carolina to Washington, D.C., while his sister had gone to his grandparents' home in California. After the trip he was putting a map puzzle together and showing how he had traveled farther than his sister, because he had gone to Washington. He mistook Washington state, however, for Washington, D.C. For years his aunt had made fun of him for this mistake. As he went back to this memory, which was a part of family lore, he recalled a part he'd left out. He'd forgotten how his father had expressed pride in him despite the mistake, because he was able to read a map at age three. Now Ed was working with church judicatory leaders who had great confidence in his ability to do difficult things (as had his father, regarding Ed being able to read a map at age three). He had, for example, been sent to a series of troubled congregations where he successfully put the pieces back together (traveling, assembling a map puzzle). The early memory contained narrative clues familiar to Ed but also clues that had been omitted—how his father was proud of him for being able to read a map at three. Now he could ask what other clues lay neglected on the cutting room floor.

It isn't easy for clergy to discern and hold on to their story, because they are subjected to many forces that try to impose narratives that don't belong to them. Will tells of a parishioner who makes a weekly visit to his office "to tell me how to run the church," he says. Will has his number and does not take in this pushy narrative. Those who want to influence or change a pastor's story are usually not so blatant, however, and their attempts are more powerful for being less easy to detect.

Jesus Affirms the Hospitality of a Peasant Village

We see in Ed's account the value of discovering a lost piece of one's personal story. And we see in Will's account the power of outside narratives that try to take away one's story. Jesus lifted up the narrative of a small peasant village and challenged the dominant stories that supported the ruling classes in first-century Palestine. These wealthy rulers—including the Romans and the cooperating Jewish religious authorities—made up ten percent of the population. The other ninety percent were peasants, who produced all the wealth through agriculture. The ruling ten percent took two-thirds of all that the peasants produced, leaving them always living from hand to mouth and never far from starvation and death.[2] The peasants were kept in their place by the dominant narrative of the authorities, which told them they deserved no better than what they had and that if they knew what was good for them they wouldn't question this setup. Jesus challenged this system, and he often used parables to do so, as he does here.

> Jesus said to them, "Suppose you have a friend who comes to you in the middle of the night and says to you, 'Friend, lend me three loaves, for a friend of mine on a trip has just shown up and I have nothing to offer him.' And suppose you reply, 'Stop bothering me. The door is already locked and my children and I are in bed. I can't get up to give you anything'—I tell you, even though you won't get up and give the friend anything out of friendship, yet you will get up and give the other whatever is needed because you'd be ashamed not to." (Luke 11:5–8)[3]

In this parable Jesus paints a picture of a remarkable peasant commitment to hospitality. Villagers faithfully welcomed traveling strangers, fed them, and gave them a place to stay. The village was so poor that each act of hospitality stretched it to the limit. They scarcely had enough to feed their own families, let alone strangers. Jesus discloses the power of this hospitality when he says that even though you won't get up and give your neighbor bread to serve the traveler out of friendship, you will do it "because you'd be ashamed not to." To refuse would be to break the village honor code of hospitality.

The story told by the elite was that because the peasants lived in such dire circumstances they should fight with one another for survival. Hospitality was a silly and extravagant practice for people in their position. The ruling class had an investment in peasants treating each other inhospitably, because it served to demoralize them. A demoralized peasantry was much easier to manipulate and exploit. To his hearers' surprise, Jesus told a parable that said their simple practice of hospitality was no small thing. It revealed the sharp contrast between their humanity and the ruthless inhumanity of the ruling class. The village practice of hospitality was a taste of the messianic banquet.[4]

Jesus was not exhorting the villagers to do something more or something different. Rather, he was telling them that their inner story already expressed the dream of God.[5] If they wanted to understand God's dream, they needed look no further than their own hospitality. This striking account expresses a major theological theme of this project: *God is constantly at work in each person's story to realize God's dream*. Jesus paid attention to a piece of the peasant story that the elite had cut out and thrown away and that the peasants themselves hardly realized was part of the dream of God.

Encountering God in Our Inner Stories

God is continually at work in one's story. A person may or may not discern this activity. We have seen, however, that when our participants had the opportunity to thoughtfully explore their inner story within a supportive community, the possibility of finding evidence of God's work in that story was substantially increased. This assumption goes against the grain of a supernaturalistic theology where God is located in another realm above and beyond the world and from which God inserts Godself from outside. Jesus doesn't visit a peasant village in order to bring God into it. He tells a parable that calls them to recognize how God is and has been at work in what they are already doing.

Jesus was a further manifestation of God's work from the beginning of creation. He did not come into the world grandly, as God's messiah, but humbly. Here he was, God's anointed, entering into the common affairs of peasant life. He entered from *within* their story, not from outside it. In a contemporary culture where the dominant theology depicts God as breaking into the world from outside, it is difficult to appreciate how the divine may be discovered *within* our stories.

As the clergy with whom we worked entered the safe, hospitable place of our group, they began telling things they couldn't tell anywhere else—accounts of dysfunctional staff members, a damning annual evaluation, a bishop they didn't trust, a judicatory demanding that they condemn homosexuality, a humiliating encounter with a finance committee about their salary, a sexual affair involving congregational leaders, their doubts about staying in ministry, their temptation to cross sexual boundaries, their state of chronic fatigue, and their journey into spiritual wilderness. They also could tell stories of success—figuring out how to deal with a thorny problem in the congregation, taking a different tack in preaching and being excited about it, experiencing transcendence as they offered pastoral care to a dying person. As they told these stories they heard the sound of their own story. One participant, a respected pastor of a growing church, spoke of his success but then added, "Success doesn't get it for me anymore." He went on to tell the story he was seeing about himself, saying how he'd achieved the goals he sought, yet he didn't feel complete or fulfilled. As the group continued to meet, he engaged his companions to help him find a different story—one that was more likely to bring him fulfillment.

Listening from an Overhearing Position

Participants learned more about their story as they were invited to take an *overhearing position* in which, after they had told a narrative without interruption, they then listened as their group discussed the account. (This usually occurred in case presentations where the telling, listening, and hearing are carefully structured. This process is fully described in the next chapter.) When participants overheard a conversation among people who had listened carefully and compassionately to their presentation, they often found things in their personal narrative that helped them resolve the problem they had reported.

Kay presented a case of her conflict with Bonita, who held a lay leadership role in the church's mission to Haiti. Bonita was at odds with Gabriel, the leader of a Haitian agency that was a partner in the congregation's mission effort. Bonita criticized Gabriel and spoke disparagingly about the congregation's mission to Haiti. Kay felt Bonita was undermining the church's mission program and was furious with her. Kay said that Bonita "is by all accounts a difficult church member who has caused a 'stir' in other areas of the church ministry prior to her being involved in global mission." Kay's strategy with Bonita was to try to control her by preventing her from spreading her criticism to other church members and by not promoting Bonita's mission trips to Haiti. After telling her story, Kay listened while the rest of the group talked to each other—not to Kay—about what they'd heard. They had heard her refer to her familiarity with Edwin Friedman's book, *Generation to Generation*, in which he advanced the idea that the best way for ministers to deal with this sort of problem is *to define themselves and stay connected to the person with whom they are in conflict*. As she overheard the conversation among the listeners, she heard them say they saw evidence that she had, in fact, started to follow Friedman's principle—turning from trying to control Bonita toward staying connected with her despite their differences. When she responded to their reflection, she said, "I hadn't thought about that, but it seems to be the case." The group picked up story fragments from the cutting room floor and offered them to the story she was telling. These pieces included the fact that she had made a shift away from trying to control Bonita to staying connected with her. This overhearing process thickened her story. Although she didn't describe this new awareness as a revelation from God, the change was actually a move from control to faith. She turned from her efforts to change Bonita and instead leaned into trusting God for future developments.

The Cutting Room Floor

In this chapter we've used the metaphor of the cutting room floor to describe how people put together a story of an event. Most of the film of the actual event ends up on the cutting room floor. What remains is our particular construction of the event, crafted by us and a host of others to fit our particular way of looking at things. The view we have presented in this chapter says that the gap between what actually happened and what we can tell about it is where narrative theory does its work. In this gap stories can be changed by going back to the cutting room floor and picking up discarded film. With this additional film, our participants could often find an alternative narrative with a different plot. In this way the group helped Ben acknowledge his leadership in organizing the community love feast, for example.

In a peasant village Jesus paid attention to their practice of hospitality and, in essence, said, "Your hospitality is a taste, a clue, that God's dream is being realized right here." As in the peasant village, God comes to us within our stories, where God is ceaselessly at work to disclose Godself to us. That inner story is a constantly unfolding plot, our autobiography in motion. The group of clergy in this project helped each other find their inner stories and tell them—making frequent trips to the cutting room floor in the process.

The Search for Your Story

How do you find your way to your own story? Most clergy are steeped in stories of the Bible, the church, history, the community, individuals, and families. In the swirl of these narratives they have little time or energy to explore their own story. The next chapter offers ways for you to discover and explore your personal story.

CHAPTER 2

How Can You Know Your Story?

Gene regularly took his turn to preach at a retirement community. His sermons were condensed versions of what he had preached to his congregation that Sunday morning. He described his sermons as academic and scripted. One Sunday evening he came to the retirement community having preached a morning stewardship message at his church. No scrap of that sermon would work. But what would work? He sat in his car with only five minutes to prepare. He came up with a familiar parable, something everyone would know. That was it. Cut loose from his usual moorings, he launched into his message without knowing where he would go. He told the story of the Prodigal Son, but when he got to the part about the older brother he was inspired to deliberately tell it wrong, saying how glad the elder brother was to see his wayward brother come home. People began to say, "No, no, that's not right. You've got it all wrong. That's not the way the story goes!" Instead of dozing off, as often happened, the residents woke up to challenge this startling error. His usual one-way sermon turned into a lively conversation, and people kept talking after the service was over. This event not only awakened his audience, but also it awakened Gene to see the story of his life as a preacher and how for years he had been preaching in an academic strait jacket.

Gene's discovery gave him a chance to ask, "Is this a story I want to continue, or do I want to change the way I preach?" He chose to change that story. His preaching began to take on a more narrative quality. For the first time he drew upon stories about himself. In one sermon he concluded by singing a familiar gospel hymn, inviting the congregation to join in.

Diana Butler Bass, who has done extensive research into vital mainline Protestant congregations, says effective pastoral leaders know their story and lead with it. They exercise "narrative leadership."[1] "Some people know stories and tell them well, but," she says, they "live without intentional connection to those stories; others simply experience the quotidian life with no reflection on larger stories of meaning. In vital mainline churches," she concludes, "leaders knew their stories and lived them—thus turning the power of narrative into a source of and resource for change."[2] Gene began to pay more attention to his own story. In fact, he spent hours with his project mentor telling that story. As he did this he began to draw on his personal narrative to make changes in his preaching and his leadership of the congregation.

In our day-to-day experience we usually don't pay much attention to the narratives that make up our life. Our stories may come into view, however, when a change occurs—something unwanted or something planned. We suffer a loss, we move from one place to another, an important relationship changes, we are faced with a demanding challenge. We bear witness to a life-changing experience by telling others about it. We write in a journal and see a hidden pattern of our life come slowly into view. Or, in Gene's case, we must suddenly improvise, because we can't follow our usual routine.

The path toward learning our story is not easy to find. We seldom find it unless we have occasion to step outside our daily trek through life. Pastors in our groups had few places to tell their unedited stories—as is likely the case for you. In their congregations the words they spoke were given considerable weight; what they said was monitored and measured, and they had to be careful what they told about themselves. In denominational gatherings with other clergy they also kept their guard up. Competition for advancement and concern that they would get labeled—too liberal, too pushy, too conservative, too inexperienced, too flawed—chilled these conversations. These were not places where they could safely express the full story that told their doubts, grievances, burdens, anxieties, hopes, and dreams. Neither could they celebrate ways they had found liberation from oppressive congregational or denominational expectations. They didn't have a place to examine the whole of their story, their story unedited.

In order to explore their narrative they needed a safe place. We provided that with a physical space separate from anyone's congregation, and it became a safe emotional space. It was *liminal* space. When they came to their group meeting they crossed a threshold from their usual daily activity and into a place where they weren't tethered to their pastoral role, where they set aside differences in status and experience, and where they agreed to protect this experience with a rule of confidentiality. Our first step toward developing this liminal space was hospitality.

Hospitality

In biblical accounts there is a mandate to offer food and drink to strangers. Food and drink open the door to hospitality, and hospitality has a spiritual dimension. Suppose in hosting strangers one entertained angels unaware. The story of Abraham and Sarah sets the biblical norm for hospitality.[4] Three strangers appear to Abraham. He runs and invites them to rest and have a little food: "Let a little water be brought, and wash your feet, and rest yourselves under the tree. Let me bring a little bread, that you may refresh yourselves, and after that you may pass on." Then he far exceeds his offer of food.

RITUAL AND LIMINAL SPACE

Anthropologist Victor Turner gives an unconventional definition of "ritual" that overturns the long-held understanding that ritual serves to maintain the status quo. He says the reverse is true. Ritual serves the purpose of changing society. Ritual is an activity in which people move from their ordinary daily life across a threshold into a state of *liminality*. In that state, normal social activities and ways of relating are suspended,[3] and people lay aside roles and statuses that ordinarily separate them from each other. In a liminal state, without their customary roles, statuses, and practices, people experience something quite different from their ordinary walk through life. They enter into a subjunctive mood.

- Not the indicative mood: "God calls us to this task."
- Not the imperative mood: "We must answer this call."
- But the subjunctive: "*What if* God is calling us to this task?"

The subjunctive mood is inclusive; everyone participates in the discernment. In this liminal space people become open to different ways of thinking, feeling, and acting. They often leave this space having been changed. And that personal change may lead to social change. (We develop the idea of liminality further in chapter four.)

He quickly orders up a feast, personally rounding up a calf for the meal. He's one hundred years old, and yet he *runs* to oversee all the details. He and Sarah offer lavish hospitality, and as it turns out they are entertaining messengers from God who announce that the narrative of their life as a childless couple will be unexpectedly changed with a birth next year.

When we launched our clergy groups we offered hospitality, but we didn't fully understand what impact it would have. Then we heard about it from the participants. They told us what it was like for them to enjoy a group where they were not the leader, weren't expected to pray, didn't have to worry about arrangements, and were protected from interruptions. Their experience resonated with biblical stories of hospitality where simple gestures of care beckoned the weary to a place of rest, the thirsty to water, and the fearful to safety. At the first meeting Will brought a bag lunch. He missed the detail that lunch would be provided. When lunch was served he smiled delightedly as he set aside his sack. He came to the next meeting with a story.

Having enjoyed the unexpected hospitality in the clergy peer group, Will had wondered what it would be like to surprise his church board with hospitality. At the next meeting, in the heat of the summer, he came early and as members arrived he offered them ice cream cones. He had different flavors and options for those who could not have sugar. He made sure everyone was included. This act took the board members back to childhood memories. It created a different climate for the meeting. Will said this meeting took on a more open and hopeful quality than typical board meetings.

It is easy to overlook the power of hospitality. Before people can speak or listen openly, they must be cherished and welcomed. That welcome must come from a deep well of acceptance and grace. "We care about you, and want to make you feel at home. Come, join us at the table."

Silence was another part of our hospitality. We began each clergy peer session with St. Benedict's practice of *lectio divina* as a ritual for entering liminal space. We read a biblical text, poem, or brief narrative three times, with silence between each reading. About silence, Kelli recalls, "When I was in the fifth grade my mom was my Sunday school teacher. One Sunday she asked the class to be silent and tell her when we thought a minute had passed. I think I lasted fifteen seconds. I could not believe how long a silent minute seemed." Leaders and participants were so unaccustomed to long periods of silence that at the beginning of the project the seconds dragged by. As we leaned in to the practice of silence, it became a gift. It created a transition from the rapid pace of daily existence to a slower and more reflective experience. It slowed down the effort at productivity and gave participants a space *to be without doing*. In this liminal space they could tell and reflect on their stories as they could not in the intensity of their day-to-day work.

As they experienced hospitality, the absence of demands, and freedom from their usual responsibilities, they could listen more thoughtfully to themselves, to each other, and to God. And they laughed. They laughed at themselves and the absurdity of their work. They poked fun at their denomination. They told stories of the stranger-than-fiction events that ministry brought to their doorstep. One participant talked about how relieved he was when he went to pay a visit and no one was home. Everyone laughed at those situations in which, by leaving their calling card, they would get "credit" for a visit in their busy day without having to spend the time doing it.

The Group Covenant

The liminal space of these clergy groups required a covenant, an understanding of mutual commitment. The covenant included: (1) Leaders and participants would respect each other's story by listening from a curious rather than a knowing position. We adopted a simple but countercultural rule from Parker Palmer's practice of Circles of Trust: "No fixing, no saving, no advising, no setting each other straight."[5] (2) As ones doing research and writing and making presentations, we the leaders covenanted that unless otherwise agreed, we would treat all information from participants as confidential. Information about them could not be shared outside the group by project participants or staff members unless the participant gave permission. Unless a participant requested otherwise, information about them could, however, be used for research purposes and for public presentations where the identity of the participant was thoroughly disguised. Our second group of clergy changed the covenant to say that leaders and other participants will seek permission *each time* they want to use another person's story. These covenants were a bedrock for group trust.

CORE ACTIVITIES FOR EXPLORING PERSONAL "STORIES OF MY LIFE"

In the course of their two-year group, we invited participants to work through the following core activities to uncover their story:

- Recall and write down your earliest childhood memory.
- Choose one of your favorite biblical narratives and ask how it may be put into conversation with your earliest childhood memory.
- Draw and present to the group a genogram (a family tree) of your family over three generations.
- Tell of an experience of being a leader before you were twenty.
- Present cases of your work as a minister using a narrative approach.
- Let us record and transcribe an interview about your life in ministry.
- From a part of that interview, carve out a poem about yourself.
- Schedule two hours a month to meet privately with a project mentor.

This chapter describes these core activities.

Early Childhood Memories

In the last chapter we noted the power of earliest childhood memories. When we asked participants to share these memories, we were asking them to pick out a narrative that was old and worn and from which many details had been lost. It was a narrative that through time had also acquired details and nuances that were not present in the original event. As they recovered the memory, they were going to the cutting room floor with glasses shaped by their present outlook on life. That meant that many other childhood stories were excluded from the search. The one they included tended to "fit" their present way of seeing the world. It was a powerful clue to their inner story.[6]

Sandra, a fifty-one-year-old minister, was one of the first women to be pastor of a congregation in her conference. During her career she had seen male pastors ascend the denominational ladder, while she was kept in low-level appointments. She complained often about hitting the glass ceiling in the system. Her earliest childhood memory was this:

My mother, baby brother, and I were on an airplane. It was a small plane, not a jet, with four seats across. We were on the right side. I was in the window seat; my mother was in the aisle seat with my brother lying across her lap. Somehow I got free and remember running down the aisle. My mother couldn't jump up and grab me because of my brother. I ran straight to the cockpit, which had a curtain instead of a door across it. I brushed by the curtain and stopped. I could see the two pilots, their backs to me, and the gray panel with all the controls. Immediately, before the pilots could even acknowledge my presence in the cockpit, a stewardess snatched me up and returned me to my seat. I then remember trying to break past my mother's knees again. But she was much more forceful in keeping me in my place.

Sandra described how she repeatedly had been held back by the denominational system. She told about her habit of complaining and described herself as "The Queen of Ain't It Awful." As she gave an account of her present appointment, however, she struck a different note. She reported that the congregation had just given her a highly favorable evaluation. She liked it so much she "wanted to frame it." She saw a contrast between her "ain't it awful" view of life and the outlook of "gratitude" she experienced in her present appointment.[7]

She said her early memory was a picture of how she felt trapped in a system that privileged men and not women. A member of the group asked Sandra whether there might be two stories in the memory and not just one. She did break loose from her mother, run to the cockpit, and open the curtain on the wonders of the pilot's cabin. What about that story? This take on the memory was a clue to an alternative narrative of her courage, resourcefulness, determination, and accomplishment. It also depicted an experience, however brief, of awe and wonder.

Weeks later Sandra was trying to come up with a biblical narrative to use as a counterpoint to her early memory. She asked her mentor for help. The mentor offered a possible connection with Moses leading the people through the desert but not being allowed into the Promised Land. She thought this fit. It not only spoke to her disappointment and grief at being held back, but it also caused her to identify with Moses as a strong leader. In a later conversation, her mentor asked her what she would most like to have said about her when she retires. She said that in writing down her early memory and account of Moses she realized that her ministry would end after forty years—just like Moses's. "I want them to say I was faithful," she said, "faithful to serve God in small churches wherever I was called. I didn't get to be pastor of a big church, but it doesn't matter. Faithfulness is what matters. If they can say that, I'll have been a success."

Sandra's early memory reflects the pain of hitting the glass ceiling, and it reveals a positive account as well. Unlike this memory, some childhood memories are quite painful, so much so that a person may not be able to tell it. It was important for us as group leaders to pay careful attention to painful memories, told or untold. We had one instance of a participant who couldn't tell an early childhood memory because of the pain of it, and we honored this reluctance. In this case it was important to provide pastoral care afterward in private conversations. These conversations gave the person a chance to consider how to deal with the recovered memory. In rare cases consultation with a therapist may be recommended.

Early Memory and a Favorite Biblical Story

Once participants identified their earliest childhood memory, a next step was choosing a favorite biblical narrative. At first group members tried to find a biblical narrative that "fit" their earliest childhood memory, as Sandra did. We learned that it's important to let that effort go and instead simply choose a biblical narrative that is a favorite. Once these two narratives have been identified, *then* ask how they may be in conversation with each other. At first there may seem to be no connection at all, yet there surely is, because each choice comes out of the same person, who has the same perspective, the same issues, the same desires and hopes. The work of relating the two stories is a creative undertaking that can yield surprises, valuable clues to one's life story, and possibilities of God's disclosure.

Family Genograms

A genogram is a drawing of family relationships that typically covers three generations: the generation of the person creating it, the generation of the family of origin, and the generation before that. The genogram has symbols showing persons and their generational connections, along with other symbols that tell of the quality of those relationships and of notable characteristics of key individuals.

We showed the participants how to construct a genogram and then turned them loose with large easel sheets and markers. It was not easy to translate their family experience into a drawing, using what for many of them were strange and esoteric symbols. As the work was being done we coached them individually, and they helped each other. We were not looking for perfect family trees. We understood that the important thing was engaging in the process and getting something down on paper. Some genograms were filled with detail, including many notes about individuals and how they did or didn't get along with certain family members. Other genograms were spare and showed little or no detail. Some drew families that were filled with difficulties—addictions, divorce, abuse, emotional cutoffs, and rivalries. Others depicted families in which "Never was heard a discouraging word."

No matter how they were drawn, the power of the genogram to disclose a person's self story came when participants presented their genograms to the group. Their presentations were "performances" of their self stories. The performance thickened the story and made it more accessible to them. As they told the story of their family over three or four generations, it opened up conversation with the group about who they were in their family network. As the group asked questions of the presenter, they were bound by the rule of not-knowing and curiosity. As presenters described their family, they experienced the power of their life story, which brought them both pain and celebration. Even those who had drawn genograms with little detail were surprised to discover that the conversation with the group revealed a richness they'd not seen.

The genogram was a medium through which they could perform their personal story by winding their way through the forest of their family. There were no "good" or "bad" genograms.

Sharon was disappointed in her genogram. She was having trouble getting the hang of it and was somewhat apologetic when she presented it. Two important narratives, however, emerged from her presentation. The first was that the genogram revealed a number of emotional cutoffs—situations where family members stopped having anything to do with other family members. A dispute would occur, followed by a refusal of the parties to communicate any further. These cutoffs extended over months and years. Emotion welled up as she began to realize how much she, her parents, and her brother had lost in these cutoffs. A second genogram story told about

> For guidance in drawing a family genogram, see the Resources section of the book for a sample genogram as well as websites that provide programs for drawing genograms.

her parents being involved in politics and how, through their influence, she became a player in political campaigns. As a young woman she became a driver and traveling companion for a woman who was running for the office of state auditor. Sharon's duties included writing speeches for the candidate. She said that these early political ventures taught her many of the skills she now uses to lead her congregation. It didn't matter that the genogram fell short of her standards for order; it enabled her to have a conversation about her family that disclosed two important dimensions of her self story—the negative influence of emotional cutoffs and the positive influence of her early political experience.

Leadership before Age Twenty

We asked participants to think of a story of their leadership before they were twenty years old—another path to access their story. In the formative period before age twenty, persons develop basic life patterns they tend to carry through the rest of their lives. In these stories they could see themselves at work as a leader but from a distance.

The group took a few minutes to write down a memory of leadership before they were twenty and then to share that recollection with the group. Here are six accounts we heard and our take on how their memory relates to their present ministry.

At age six *Sadie* wanted a bicycle, and she just couldn't wait until Christmas to get it. So she organized a neighborhood carnival, involving her older siblings and their friends to help her pull it off. She raised enough money to buy the bike. In her ministry Sadie became a project organizer and leader—taking young people on mission trips in the United States and abroad to serve marginalized populations and to assist in disaster recovery. She became the chaplain to a denominational college—exercising her organizing ability to establish a comprehensive ministry to students, faculty, and staff.

In high school *Will* made a highly organized presentation to the student body to persuade them to have as a prom theme "Carolina Moon." He got overwhelming support from his fellow students, although the teachers thought it was a bad idea. In his ministry he has challenged persons in authority positions on justice issues. During the project he was invited to join a support group of older clergy who held prominent places of leadership in the denomination past and present—all of them white males. He talked with his clergy group about his dilemma. He felt he couldn't join a group of clergy that was all-male, all-white, and closed to considering persons with other sexual orientations. He was told by a representative of that group that he could join as long as he had "no agenda." He chose to stick by his "agenda" that he couldn't join a group that did not permit women, persons of other races, or gay or lesbian persons to join. Thereby he eliminated himself from membership.

In high school *Ed* said no to the swimming coach who wanted to use him as a replacement for a member of the swim relay team, after the relay team had already qualified for a swim meet. He thought it was not right for him to replace a team member after the team had qualified. In his denomination he became a mentor to other clergy and often extended himself to care for ministers in difficulty—championing their welfare when no one else did. Although it was difficult, he got the denomination to provide care for a minister who suffered a disabling emotional illness.

In the fifth and sixth grades, *Evelyn* was given responsibility to be the student head of the school library. She developed an effective check-out system, replacing one that didn't work. She took criticism from the students, however, because they didn't like the way she reminded them about overdue books. She came from a family, she said, that thrived on intellectual debate, competition, and an ongoing contest to be "right." With her clergy peers she was able to see that her family story of being right got in the way of building relationships in the group and in her congregation.

As an older teenager *Kathy* and another camp counselor, both of whom were not much older than their camp charges, took the group down the river on a canoe outing. They missed the poorly marked pick-up point and continued until they were almost at the Mississippi River. She ended up driving a flat-bed truck full of campers and hauling a trailer of canoes. She'd never driven a truck before. In her ministry Kathy has assumed a role as a community leader beyond her congregation, often taking risks that others were reluctant to take.

Alice, at age fourteen, took the initiative to propose a different kind of play at church—more elaborate than had been done before, using projection on a back-lighted screen. Today she is an innovator in worship and congregational ministries. She initiated programs in her parish on faith and science and on faith and the arts—securing outside grants to help support them.

Case Presentations

Evelyn was dismissed as the minister of her congregation shortly after she joined our first clergy group. She felt like the one unsuccessful minister in a group of successful ones. Ben was pastor of a large and fast-growing congregation in the area. She perceived him as being adored by his flock. He was at the top of her list of the successful ones, and she envied him. Then one day Ben told the group his story of depression and despair. He had been brought low by a group in the congregation that did not respect him and that tried to undermine his leadership at every turn—specifically at the point of derailing a much-needed capital campaign. He was at his wits end and thinking about leaving the ministry. Evelyn had thought he couldn't be touched by the kind of trouble she'd been through. As she overheard this story, however, she learned that he was suffering with trouble like hers. She felt less like "the failed one" and more like a fellow sufferer.

Ben did not try to directly encourage, support, or help Evelyn in her suffering, although he is a caring and supportive person. Neither he nor others in the group could really see Evelyn's shame. It was hidden from view. But when she overheard his story it touched her.

An overhearing experience provides the listener with both distance and participation. Evelyn could sit safely distant from Ben as he told the story of his suffering as the leader of a growing congregation. That gave her room to reflect, accept, reject, or wonder. She was under no pressure to apply anything Ben said to her own life. Given this distance, however, she was able freely to choose to allow Ben's story to touch hers. In this freedom she was drawn into his story and into her own hidden suffering.[8]

OVERHEARING

Jesus was a master at placing people in an overhearing position. Consider his parables—the prodigal son, the good Samaritan, the laborers in the vineyard, the talents, the friend at midnight, and others. He gives no direct address, no exhortation, no explanation. The audiences overhear a parable and are perplexed as these stories subvert their familiar way of seeing the world.

Overhearing combines *distance* and *participation*. Distance offers the hearer room to reflect, accept, wonder, imagine—things for which there is little room in direct address. Listeners are full participants, yet their participation is markedly different from participation in direct speech and hearing.[9] A movie or play is an overhearing experience. People are addressed indirectly as someone else's story is played out before them. When the first performance of his play "The Death of a Salesman" ended, Arthur Miller said there was nothing but silence. He and the cast held their breaths. In the silence, as one actor observed, "Extremely sophisticated very successful New Yorkers with absolutely no questions at all about who they are, how far they've come, and how right their lives are . . . dissolve[d] in tears, their shoulders shaking." Then there was a swell of sustained applause. The audience and the cast had *overheard* the story of Willy Lowman. Elizabeth Franz, who played Willy's wife, wept so desperately at the end of the play that when the curtain call came she was still shaking with sobs.[10] Could direct speech produce such transforming moments?

Our case presentation method provided a structured process for teaching participants the value of overhearing. At each meeting someone presented a case—a narrative about a situation in which consultation was needed. Case presentations took an hour and followed this structure: The presenter chose a conversation partner and told the case story to that partner. The rest of the group formed a reflecting team[11] that listened to the presenter-partner dialogue without interruption. An invisible barrier separated the reflecting team from the presenter and partner, and there was no cross talk between them.

So how does such listening and reflecting unfold? The presenter tells the listening partner the story of the case for twenty minutes, speaking to the partner as if no one else is present. The partner's responsibilities are, first, to listen with curiosity, from time to time asking clarifying questions, and second, to ask questions that focus on the inner world of the presenter more than on the person or persons being reported on.

The reflecting team members heed the boundary between themselves and the presenter-partner dyad, and they do not speak. They pay attention to the presenter as storyteller. The presenter and partner do not speak to them.

Following the presentation the case facilitator asks for one minute of silence, allowing the conversation to come to rest, keeping the pace deliberate, and giving the reflecting team time to ponder what they have heard.

For the next fourteen minutes the reflecting team members talk among themselves about what they have heard. The boundary is maintained between the reflecting team and the presenter-partner dyad, and the presenter and partner remain silent. Members of the reflecting team do not speak to the presenter or partner, only to each other. The reflecting team takes a curious, not-knowing stance. They do not try to analyze, diagnose, fix, judge, or advise the presenter. They speak briefly to each other, do not make long speeches, and more often than not ask questions of other reflecting team members. They pay attention to *the presenter as storyteller*. They may note briefly their own experience that relates to the presenter's story.

They avoid a deficiency-oriented stance and instead maintain a *relentless optimism*.

Next, presenter and partner take ten minutes to respond to what they have heard the reflecting team say. The boundary between the dyad and the reflecting team is held firm. The focus of this dialogue is on the reflecting team conversation and how it has affected the presenter.

The partner's task here is to help the presenter focus on what the reflecting team has

RELENTLESS OPTIMISM

Relentless optimism is a term we've borrowed from narrative therapy to express our theological view that God is constantly at work in our personal and collective stories to realize God's dream for us. Although we may not pay attention to this ongoing work, it's there nonetheless—God's persistent, compassionate presence. This belief connects with our conviction that God is always at work to offer an alternative narrative.

Relentless optimism does not ignore the negative power of the problem story and the ways the presenter is trapped in that story. These must be taken into account or the "optimism" is a thoughtless attempt to give useless encouragement.

said and what she or he has learned from them. The partner often leads with the question, "What did you hear from the reflecting team?" The partner pays attention to the presenter's emotion and follows these feelings. Attention to strong emotion may move the conversation beyond what the reflecting team has said.

Finally, the boundary is removed and all speak together for the remainder of the hour. The removal of the boundary changes the conversation so that all participants can talk about the content and the process of the case presentation. If there are observers beyond the reflecting team, this is an opportunity for them to comment on the process.

The reflecting team works best when the boundaries and time limits are carefully maintained. This structure increases emotional safety for the presenter and the participants. The element of competition diminishes. People are more willing to risk vulnerability. To present a problem to a group without clear structures can be an intimidating and unnerving experience. The presenter doesn't know what's going to happen next; and there's too much opportunity for intrusive, critical, judgmental, not curious, or otherwise inappropriate questions.

When the reflecting team process is unclear, safety is diminished. If the time boundaries are unclear or ignored, the container is weakened. Paradoxically, firm boundaries increase rather than diminish the freedom of the conversation. Because the boundaries and the time are held firm, presenters experience a safety that allows them to risk greater self-disclosure. Carrying out this form of case presentation requires practice in order for people to retrain themselves not to follow the conventional wisdom of acting like experts, assuming to know what's happened, and offering advice. The mandate for the reflecting team is, "Do your best to try not to fix anything."

Dick observes, "On occasion I have asked a group to enter into a reflecting team form of conversation without preparing them ad-

ONE-HOUR CASE PRESENTATION SCHEDULE	
Minutes	Activity
20	The presenter tells the story of the case to the partner.
1	Silence.
14	The reflecting team members talk among themselves while presenter and partner overhear.
10	The presenter responds to the reflecting team, speaking only to the partner, who helps the presenter stay focused on what the reflecting team has said.
15	The boundary between the reflecting team and the presenter-partner dyad is removed, and everyone talks together.

equately for this countercultural way of talking. The results have been confusing. After a couple of these failures I learned that you cannot launch into this kind of conversation without carefully preparing the group." The preparation amounts to the development of a covenant with the group about trying something new and perhaps awkward. This covenant is a container in which people are more likely to take a risk to be more open to each other and to God's spirit. One participant in our project called this "holy listening."

The structure of the case presentation, and following the basic rule of "no fixing, no saving, no advising, no setting each other straight," provides the security necessary for people to have conversations that are marked by uncertainty, not having an answer, not fixing what is askew, and not having expert knowledge. Instead, participants are taken up into stories of difficulty and impasse where the direction is not clear. The conversation structure fosters curiosity about these narratives and a search for small clues to alternative narratives, those narrative pieces on the cutting room floor that tell how presenters have solved other problems, been courageous, acted with wisdom, and become aware of God's work in their lives. Even the smallest piece of evidence of an alternative story is significant and can be thickened by finding other similar, small narrative fragments. No fragment is too small to make a difference.

Those who have practiced the reflecting team method of case presentations often comment that the experience is not a routine but an event. Presenters go away from the event surprised at the support they felt and by what they learned about themselves. What gives this practice such power? The presenter, the conversation partner, and the reflecting team take a not-knowing position. They set aside the practice of analyzing a problem and applying a solution. They do not quickly presume to understand the situation or the presenter. As participants take a not-knowing position, they invite surprise and epiphany, because they are not hell-bent on analyzing and figuring it all out. The presenter's story may be filled with pain and seemingly insurmountable problems, but this structure keeps anxiety in check. Hope is generated through humor and by people identifying with the presenter. Presenters are able to laugh at their own foibles, and the process often takes a playful direction.

Linking the *not-knowing position* and *the overhearing position* is a potent combination. One reinforces the other. Because no one presumes to *know* what is going on, they wonder and ask curious questions. Rather than receiving recommendations about how to solve the problem, presenters hear questions that cause them to reflect on themselves and how their own story is being disclosed in this situation. Will describes this experience, saying,

When pastors like me begin to realize that the heart of excellence is transformation of the soul, then we can make some theological connections with a God whose creative purposes are continual. We often entered the "unknown" of our lives and the lives of others in the group without judging, without advising, and without solving. The ministry of presence to one another, of walking together in the darkness, seemed to bring light out of the abyss of the unknown. Such an experience speaks volumes to me as a pastor about the multitude of abysses we enter. No pastor can have the answer to every problem that comes up. The greater realization is that I don't *have* to have the answer, but I do need to be present and faithful as I walk with my members through their "unknowns."

Interviews and Poetic Analysis

As another strategy to help participants tell their story, we interviewed each one. The interviews were recorded and transcribed; each participant received a transcript of her or his interview. Interviewers asked participants, "Tell me about your life in ministry." And they did. Some interviews ran to more than twenty single-spaced pages.

Although our process called for someone to do the tedious work of transcription, this isn't essential for doing interviews. Members of a group can take turns being interviewed using a reflecting team structure.

Interviews provided the fullest account of participants' self stories. Their stories often took them by surprise. They told of their call to ministry, their education, their different ministry positions, their families, their doubts, their fears, their aspirations, their theological struggles.

We instructed the transcriber to include all the pauses, false starts, and mistakes, so we would have a transcript that was as close as possible to the actual interview. Here is a fragment of Kay's interview. The interviewer has just asked her to elaborate on her interest in urban ministry:

Um, yeah, well, uh (pause) while I was in seminary, you know, my brother died and he was living in an urban area, and he sometimes was homeless, 'cause sometimes he would kind of lose his way, because he suffered from a severe form of schizophrenia (pause) and so I think, his kind of, you know, living in San Francisco and (pause) and being one of those people that's challenged and kind of gets lost in the system, in the city (pause), and he died while I was in seminary, and (pause) so that's one of my, you know, my convergences. I mean, I think, you know, being involved in outreach ministry as mission was always there, because it was such a big focus for the conservative churches I grew up in, but the more social justice, kind of broader awareness to the world's way of looking at it, that I felt over time, also intersected with my brother's lost place in the world (pause), and so when I wrote my dissertation, you know, I, I did speak to him.

In order to draw out more of the power of each interview, we showed participants how to take a block of material from the interview and make a poem out of it. Social researchers who use this method refer to it as "poetic analysis."[12] We asked participants to select a segment of the interview that was particularly important to them and to make a poem out of it by removing words until they had a poem. No words were changed or reordered. It was somewhat like chiseling a carving out of a piece of rough stone. Kay chose the material above as the substance for her poem. (The poem continues through some material that's not included in the section above.)

Homeless

While I was in seminary
my brother died.
Homeless,
sometimes he would lose his way,
suffered schizophrenia,
living in San Francisco,

lost in the system,
in the city,
he died.

Convergence.
Mission, outreach,
churches I grew up in,
social justice,
broader awareness,
    intersected
my brother's lost place in the world.

My dissertation.
I did speak to him,
    tied in
homelessness,
theological perspective,
sociological perspective,
analyzing,
a phenomena,
a cliché,
people displaced,
minimum wage,
housing prices.

God's presence in suffering.
Always,
always the plea
take care of homeless
in your midst,
because you were once homeless,
wandering,
God in the exile.

Kay had not looked at this poem for months when we asked her if we could use it for this chapter. When she read it again she said, "I had forgotten how powerful it is."

You may not have the option of doing transcriptions of interviews, but you can still do poetic analysis on material you've written using journal entries, letters, e-mails, sermons, newsletter columns, and the like.

Mentoring

In addition to the group work we did, we gave participants up to two hours a month of individual time with a mentor. Mentors were Kelli, Dick, and three seasoned staff members at Triangle Pastoral Counseling. In mentoring we were careful to avoid an expert model—the knowing expert who helps a minister who needs direction. We respected the wisdom of the participants and acknowledged that we were learning along with them. Our mentoring offered participants individual companionship with a person who was not connected to their congregation or denominational hierarchy. Mentors provided a safe, confidential place for them to tell their unedited stories of life in ministry. Will sent this e-mail to his mentor when she had to cancel a session due to a sick child.

You are quite lucky to miss spending an hour with me today. I'm a Grinch and Christmas cynic. Would probably just ruin your holiday. But, hey, I can do that by e-mail! But I'm not gunna. After all, it's the "most wonderful time of the year!" (Who wrote that song?!)

Actually, I prefer June 25! Things are going ok. Just little things this week like a daughter's speeding ticket, an associate with morning sickness (24 hrs. a day), another associate with vertigo, a depressed secretary, a janitor who broke down in tears during the singing of "I'll Be Home for Christmas" at the Advent luncheon yesterday, a budget that is falling short, and three thousand announcements about "special" Christmas events—to be made between the two choral anthems, the dedication of the shoe boxes for needy at-risk kids, and the lighting of the Advent wreath. And then there's the mission moment for our global offering. And please remember to thank the people who decorated the sanctuary with the beautiful fake greens and electric candles they pulled out of the storage closet again this year. And do it all in 60 minutes (50 at the 8:45 service). Sermon? Forget it! Did I mention the upcoming intervention with an alcoholic? Did I mention a grumpy and cynical pastor? Remind me that no one is forcing me to do this job! I asked for it. And as I read back on this stuff, some of it actually is a little bit funny.

(Phone rings! It's you. Thanks for checking in.) Don't worry about rescheduling any time soon. We'll work on that later between the living nativity (new and improved this year—we're using REAL fire! Help!) and the debate over live candles vs. battery candles for the Christmas Eve Service.

> Peace on earth,
> Will

Could Will freely recite this litany of woe, even tongue-in-cheek, in his congregation? No. Could he do it with other clergy in his denomination? Not likely. He needed an audience outside the congregation to hear his fatigue and weariness with the whole scene of the congregation's Christmas operetta. That audience was his mentor. She could hear it, appreciate it, laugh with him, and hold it in confidence. What a relief!

We wondered what would happen when clergy had personal time with a mentor. There's no clear answer, for each experience was unique. Some participants, like Will, thrived on mentoring. Others didn't find it that helpful. Each mentoring situation was a dance that mentor and mentee had to learn together. Some partners enjoyed the dance and some didn't.

Some mentees used their mentoring time to rehearse their story in detail. In these rehearsals they were able to piece together different parts of their narrative, often gathering up forgotten film from the cutting room floor, to get a clearer view of who they were and where they were headed. When Dorothea's mentor invited her to tell about her call to ministry, Dorothea was silent. The mentor asked what she was thinking. She said, "I'm trying to decide whether to tell you the new member inquirers' class version or the uncut version." The mentor asked for the uncut version. Dorothea said, "It came out of nowhere. I'm in a bar watching a strip show. I'm being entertained and all of a sudden something stirs over my spirit. I started crying. I'm very clear I am being called to found this church. No doubt about that. So when some kind of stupid stuff happens at the church I have to remind myself of the fact that God called me into this and God will give me what I need to get me out of this."

Mentoring did not occur just between mentor and mentee. The group itself provided mentoring, particularly when a person presented a case and heard the reflecting team's response. Participants called each other for consultation and exchanged e-mails about perplexing professional and personal challenges they faced.

Finding Your Story and Then?

We said at the beginning of this chapter that clergy who lead effectively know their story and lead with it. We've described the ways our project invited participants to find and tell their stories:

- Recall your earliest childhood memory and relate that to a biblical narrative.
- Draw and present to the group a genogram of your family over three or four generations.
- Tell about an experience of leadership before you were twenty.
- Present cases from your work as a minister.
- Tell your story of "My Life in Ministry."
- Select a section of that transcript (or some other personal written material) and carve out a poem about yourself.
- Enter a mentor-mentee relationship for a more personal place to rehearse your story.

Each of these strategies helped participants get a clearer picture of their story.

The title of our book is *Know Your Story and Lead with It*. What is the relationship between knowing your story and leadership? How are these two things related? That's where we turn in the next chapter.

CHAPTER 3 |
Narrative Leadership

When we began this project our stated purpose was "to help pastors of congregations overcome the isolation of their role, to develop an integrated view of pastoral work, and to become mentors to other pastors to help them overcome pastoral isolation and role fragmentation." The further we got into the project, the more we realized that we and the participants were engaged in an effort to nurture *narrative leadership*—a development we didn't expect.

Our emerging understanding of narrative leadership is based on the idea that more than one story can be told about any person or event. When people see themselves at a dead end, that's only one story about the situation. "There's no way to move forward with this building project. The cost has gone far beyond what we can pay." That's one story. A minister with a narrative orientation might respond, "It's true, we are up against a perplexing problem. I wonder whether there are other stories we can play out? What has the congregation done in other situations that looked like dead ends?" Individuals and congregations construct narratives to make sense of their situation; however, other narrative possibilities exist and usually lie hidden from view. These are the narrative fragments we have described as lying on the cutting room floor. Narrative leaders know how to go looking for these other stories. This narrative approach invites curiosity in individuals and groups about the unfolding plot of their situation and prompts them to make conscious choices between plots they prefer and plots they don't. Narrative leaders become conscious agents of change—intentional authors of their own stories. And they invite others to examine story plots and how they can change those plots to move beyond "This is the same old story."

The story about Alice getting hit by a car told in chapter one demonstrates how many different stories can be told by eyewitnesses to an event. After hearing the different accounts of the accident, Will said, "These are all different narratives. Each story constructs reality; we'll never recover what *actually* happened." He's exactly right. All that could be recovered from the event were our varying reconstructions of it. And our individual stories about the event were influenced by many circumstances, including our vantage point, what was already on our mind, our typical way of responding to an emergency, our relationship to others involved, and what grabbed our attention in a fast-moving event. Narrative leaders—in this case you as a clergy leader—understand this phenomenon and keep the door open to alternatives others may not see.

Looking for a Role Model of Narrative Leadership

As we looked for role models that demonstrated a narrative way of leading, we "met Jesus again for the first time"[1] to see that he practiced a form of narrative leadership. He delivered his message through stories, and he challenged the prevailing narratives of power and privilege, as the Hebrew prophets did before him. He affirmed the little narratives of hope among the peasants against the grand narratives of domination of the ruling classes. In short, he led through narrative.

As a narrative practitioner, Jesus challenged conventional wisdom. Conventional wisdom is a culture's way of seeing the world that gives advantage to those in power and defends the social status quo. People internalize this "wisdom" and live out of it, unless they are able to see a different kind of wisdom. Marcus Borg identifies these characteristics of conventional wisdom: It domesticates reality for the convenience of those in power. It is based on reward and punishment. It is a world of hierarchy and boundaries. It produces a life of anxious striving and conformity. The spell of conventional wisdom produces self-preoccupation and selfishness. Conventional wisdom views God as a lawgiver and judge and sees the religious life as a set of demanding requirements. Conventional wisdom is not confined to a particular society or time; it pervades all traditions.[2]

Jesus spoke of conventional wisdom as "the broad way" and God's wisdom as "a narrow way."[3] He depicted God not as a judge but as a compassionate being who offered cosmic generosity. He spoke of the kingdom of God in parables that described God's kingdom as a place populated by marginalized people—nobodies— not by those with wealth and power.[4] Jesus was repeatedly criticized for being host to meals that included sinners and tax collectors. These meals were enacted parables of inclusion that subverted the conventional wisdom of privilege, purity, and exclusion.[5]

The wisdom of narrative leadership subverts the wisdom of establishment power. The conventional wisdom of establishment power says, "This is the way the world is. Accept it." Conventional wisdom uses its tools of persuasion, including religious justification, to convince those without power that their condition is what they deserve and is all they should expect. Jesus's wisdom says an emphatic no to this story. His approach to conventional wisdom challenges any story—individual or cultural—to answer the questions: Does this story serve the well-being of people or does it pose a barrier to their well-being? Does it reflect God's justice and mercy? Does it express God's generous compassion?

If Jesus's transformative leadership challenged conventional wisdom with God's unconventional wisdom, as did the prophets before him, then it follows that clergy today are summoned to an unconventional leadership despite the fact that pursuit of an unconventional wisdom involves greater risks than staying within the safety of conventional thought and practice.

A contemporary role model for our view of narrative leadership is Parker Palmer. His book *A Hidden Wholeness* has been a resource in our thinking about narrative leadership. He writes:

What sort of space gives us the best chance to hear soul truth and follow it? A space defined by principles and practices that honor the soul's nature and needs. What is that nature, and what are those needs? My answer draws on the only metaphor I know that reflects the soul's essence while honoring its mystery: the soul is like a wild animal.

Like a wild animal, the soul is tough, resilient, resourceful, savvy, and self sufficient: it knows how to survive in hard places. . . .

Yet, despite its toughness, the soul is also shy. Just like a wild animal, it seeks safety in the dense underbrush, especially when other people are around. If we want to see a wild animal, we know that the last thing we should do is go crashing through the woods yelling for it to come out.

Unfortunately, *community* in our culture too often means a group of people who go crashing through the woods together, scaring the soul away. . . . We scare off all the soulful things, like respectful relationships, goodwill, and hope.[6]

If you are a minister, you contend with endless expectations to have answers for people's problems. You are under constant pressure to solve congregational problems and are beseeched by parishioners to fix their personal lives. Because of this pressure, it can be hard for you to hear a problem without posing a solution. Obviously there are times when a ready answer is needed; however, you have to do the hard work of discernment to keep from slipping into the exhausting practice of constant fixing and giving answers.

In groups he calls "circles of trust," Palmer counters these natural human inclinations with "profoundly countercultural" norms: "Thou shalt not even *try* to save each other!" This injunction goes against "the gravitational field of conventional culture" that pulls us toward "invasive ways of relating." People resist this different norm, saying, "Saving each other is why we were put here on earth!"[7] Against this he posts the rule, now familiar to you, of "no fixing, no saving, no advising, no setting each other straight." We put this rule on the wall as a constant reminder to us and our participants to stay curious and avoid trying to save each other. It's a difficult rule to follow. We and our participants often got caught up in the spiral of problem solving. We were saved from this when someone asked, "Are we staying curious or are we trying to fix something?" Trying to fix problems that people report is a seductive circumstance in which we hear a siren call to come running with our evaluation, advice, admonition, examples, and directions.

Leadership and Not-Knowing

The rule of "no fixing, no saving, no advising, no setting each other straight" places people in a curious, not-knowing position. It may seem strange to link the word *leadership* to *not-knowing*. Our cultural images of leaders are of those who know, explain, and command. Linking *leadership* to *not-knowing* would appear to be the script for weak and ineffective leaders. But is this so?

One definition of not-knowing means "I don't know, I'm lost, I'm in the dark." We typically refer to a person in this state as "clueless." This understanding of not-knowing is related to characteristics such as lack of insight, being unprepared, incompetence, lack of attention, or not caring about the situation.

The definition of not-knowing used in this project means taking a humble stance toward what one knows rather than promoting or validating one's own knowledge. It means setting aside certainty and being open to learn. Not-knowing means suspending knowledge and expertise in order to hear something new, something different, something that would not be heard if one moved forward knowingly. This kind of not-knowing is driven not so much by a search for the truth but by a desire to understand. Leaders who take this not-knowing approach rely on curious questions. Their questions grow out of the stories they hear from an individual or group. They do not presume to know what's going on within a group or a person. They are continually learning from the person, group, or congregation.[8]

The minister says to a church member, "You said you were disappointed that I didn't do more to lead vacation Bible school this year. I would like to know more about your view. What did you want to see me doing that you didn't see?" A follow-up question: "If I had done what you wanted to see, how would that have changed the experience for you?" Another question: "Are there other things that you feel need to be different?" This minister is able to move beyond justifying her behavior to being curious. It is possible that her curious questions will allow the congregant to tell about a more personal issue than his displeasure with her.

Moving from Grand Strategy to Not-Knowing

Statement A: *"Being a pastor is like playing chess. I always need to be thinking three moves ahead."*

Statement B: *"I am learning that leadership is being enough in front to see a next good step. It's not always being at the destination before everyone else has left home."*

These two statements are from the same pastor. Statement A comes from the beginning of Jim's participation in the project. Statement B comes near the end of his two years in the project. In the interim the metaphor has changed from a chess game made up of strategic moves to stay ahead of the congregation to a journey on which pastor and congregation travel together.

Jim faced the challenge of a capital project that involved renovating and expanding all the church buildings except the sanctuary. The cost was projected at $4 million. Jim supported this emerging plan but struggled with "how to build consensus in a congregation that wasn't entirely sold on attempting such a large project." He wanted to take the lead "without being manipulative or coercive," and he wondered how he could exercise spiritual leadership in the process.

He devised a story-telling plan. He arranged a congregational meeting where people who had led earlier building projects, including the pastor emeritus and the chair of the last building committee, told their stories. They didn't make pre-planned statements. Jim asked a newspaper reporter who was a member of the congregation to interview them, and the congregation overheard their conversation. One couldn't predict what would come out of that free-flowing interaction. Following these accounts Jim invited members "to say anything on their heart" about the building proposal. He established ground rules. There would be no discussion of the merits of the statements. Speakers would express their hopes and concerns, and then their comments would "rest" with the congregation in silence before the moderator moved to the next speaker. At the close of the meeting, members were given two blank note cards. On one card they could state their concerns and on the other card what excited them about the project. The cards were collected and posted on a bulletin board for all members to read and ponder.

Jim said, "I think I was led in this direction due to some insights drawn from the clergy group I am in. Answers aren't always your goal. Sometimes the true genius is in helping people discover a healthy process to reach decisions. The risk is people may not decide what you want. The reward is that if they do come to other conclusions in a healthy manner, you can live with the decisions with a greater degree of integrity than if you fought for a goal and came up on the short end of the stick. There is also the very real possibility that you may be wrong and a process you trust can help you see your own fallibility."

The heavy expectation that we ministers should be knowers is fuel for anxiety. If we have to be knowers, then we live with

---

ABRAHAM LINCOLN AND NOT-KNOWING

When he gave his second inaugural address on March 4, 1865, near the close of the Civil War, Abraham Lincoln assumed a not-knowing position. It had become clear that the North would win the war, and this success had guaranteed Lincoln's election to a second term. When he stood to deliver his inaugural address, people expected a victory speech, but they didn't get it. They got instead a brief speech of 703 words in which he set aside certainty and blame and turned instead to the mystery of God's providence, saying, "Each looked for an easier triumph and a result less fundamental and astounding. Both read the same Bible, and pray to the same God; and each invokes His aid against the other. It may seem strange that any men should dare to ask a just God's assistance in wringing their bread from the sweat of other men's faces; but let us judge not that we be not judged. The prayers of both could not be answered; that of neither has been answered fully. The Almighty has His own purposes."[9]

the anxiety that we'll be caught not-knowing. It's not unusual for this anxiety to speak with an inner voice that says, "One of these days they'll find out you are a fraud, because so often you've acted knowingly when you didn't know." This anxiety begins to subside when we ministers can take a not-knowing position. Then we can face situations not as a hero but as a partner with the congregation. Instead of fearing we'll be found out to be not-knowing, we choose it as a key to wise leadership.

Once released from the anxious state of always being knowers, we clergy are able to listen to the inner wisdom of our own story. We then are able to listen to the stories of others. And we are more open to hearing God's story—how God may be speaking to us in our stories and the stories of other people.

Hierarchy and Curiosity

This is what we learned: When you take a not-knowing position you are recognizing your limits, your finitude. You cannot understand a person, a group, or an institution all on your own. You have to learn from others, and you can only do this if you remain curious. Curiosity toward others is enabled by your curiosity toward yourself. There is a reciprocal relationship between having a curious, not-knowing stance toward others and having such a stance toward yourself. In fact, genuine curiosity toward others' stories is grounded in curiosity about your own.

In the book's introduction, Dick described his difficulty in making the transition from being a professor to a group leader in the project. About that he says,

> In order for me to understand why I wasn't doing so well co-leading our clergy groups early in this project I had to be curious about my own story. I asked, "Why isn't this working like it used to when I was teaching?" Kelli saw the situation more clearly than I could. She viewed it from her perspective as a parish minister. She was professionally and emotionally closer to our clergy group than I was. She saw that I was assuming my accustomed professor's position.

With her help I began to re-examine my story as a teacher and saw that I had lost professorial power. As a professor I had developed a teaching method that involved students leading other student groups in my classes, and I supervised these group leaders. It was a partnership, and it mitigated the traditional hierarchical teaching model. Yet I always held the trump card of the grade and course credit.

I had to revise my story, but I didn't do it in isolation. The revision occurred in a community that let me know the professor story didn't fit. My story revision had the effect of making me more curious. I found that as hierarchy is reduced, curiosity tends to increase.

Dick's story of disorientation has an affinity with the account of James and John asking Jesus to give them privileged positions of power—to sit on his right hand and on his left hand in his "glory." When the other ten disciples got wind of this they were "indignant." Jesus told all of them, "You know among the gentiles those they call their rulers lord it over them, and their great men make their authority felt. Among you this is not to happen. No; anyone who wants to become great among you must be your servant, and anyone who wants to be first among you must be slave to all. For the Son of man himself came not to be served but to serve."[10] He challenged the disciples' desire for privilege and power. Jesus's way was leadership *with* and not leadership *from above*. He reversed the cultural leadership story that said leaders dominate their subjects. His way was to enter into the world of the powerless to say that God breaks the yoke of oppression and that God does not come to them through a domination system but around a table that is open to everyone.

It is difficult for persons to tell you what they believe, think, and feel if you operate from a position of power over them. From such a knowing position, it is difficult to muster genuine curiosity, because you might hear things that challenge that power-over position. This news could get in the way of your plans as a leader. As a result you are deprived of vital information that you need. Domination and lack of curiosity have their price.

Leadership from a not-knowing position runs counter to our cultural norms for leadership, which say that good leaders take charge and lead out of their own ideas and visions. Followers respond by making a choice to get on board with the leader or not. These leaders are not interested in the stories of those they lead, because they believe the really important story is the one they are writing from above. In contrast, clergy who operate out of a narrative perspective lead *beside,* not from above. Leading beside others means, first, that they understand their own story and, second, that they learn from the narratives of those they lead. As they do this, they join their followers as a partner and not a superior.

Gene was well trained in the take-all-the-responsibility and give-people-answers mode; it was engrained in him. He was deeply distressed about the behavior of his associate, who was making inappropriate references to intimate matters of his personal life in worship services and was verbally blundering across sexual boundaries. Gene made heroic efforts to help the associate, but it wasn't working. This problem pushed Gene's anxiety higher and higher. Finally he admitted that he couldn't repair the situation. He turned to the church board for help, admitting he didn't know what to do next. To his immense relief, they assumed responsibility for direct supervision of the associate. Gene got the help he needed from the board when he admitted to not-knowing.

Months later Gene thickened this story of not-knowing with a story of not-fixing. A group of people was gathered in the hall asking who was going to put up the vacation Bible school sign in front of the church. They all looked to him—he who kept a toolbox in his office for just such occasions. He thought to himself, "I'm not going to do it. I'm tired of doing things that aren't in my job description." With a brief comment to the group, he walked away. He said that every inch of his body resisted turning away. His stomach was tied in a knot. A part of him believed, yes, he should go hang that vacation Bible school sign, but another part of him said, "No, don't do it. Here is a place not to be helpful." So, later someone else put up the sign. His inward agony of turning away from the task others were expecting him to do was the result of a new story of paying attention to his limits and leading by letting go—which enables others to take responsibility. This account illustrates how a small event can bring about important change. Gene was tempted, as most clergy would be, simply to do the job. It would be easy and wouldn't ruffle feathers. He'd often done tasks that belonged to others. This small act of not helping contributed to rewriting his story and setting it in a not-knowing direction—as well as launching others into a narrative of "Let's do it ourselves."

Narrative Leadership and the Clergy Terminator

Owen had been instrumental in firing the last two pastors, and a legend had grown up around him that he held a Sword of Damocles over the head of any minister in that church. Larry, the associate pastor, presented this case of his encounter with Owen.

My day began with an e-mail from Owen that read: "Larry, I would like to meet with you about some things I have been hearing. Could we do it in the next few days?" Though this sounds benign enough, I felt a sinking feeling in my stomach. Owen never wants simply to "meet." I suspected that all the venom that was being spit at Frank, the senior minister, was going to find a new place to land, and I feared that my time had finally come. What has nagged me about this particular conflict between Frank, Owen, and nameless "others" has been the question, "What is being said about me?" I've grown tired of being used as ammunition against Frank, but I hated even more the idea of being a target.

With just a few hours before Owen was to arrive, I was in a near panic, because I was sure this would not end well. Nothing that Owen had been involved in lately had ended in anything but discord, disappointment, hurt feelings, or threats. I called Kelli and got her reading on the situation. I called my mentor and got his consultation. After two hours of preparation, these were the things that stayed with me: Owen is coming to my office, my "house"; find strength in "my space." Though the prevailing narrative is that Owen makes life harder, listen intently for the alternative story. Remain curious. This is not a time to explain, justify, or defend anything he brings to the table. Set a time limit so that we know when to stop.

Soon enough, it was time to welcome Owen to my office. He told me that he had been hearing some things I'd probably want to hear about. Pretty benign things, really. It took five minutes, and none of them really felt all that dangerous or damaging. I asked him, "What do you want out of this conversation? What's motivating you to bring this to me now?" For the next fifty minutes he talked about his experience in the church lately. Sometimes it sounded like a plea for support, sometimes a political stump speech, sometimes an apology for the self-righteousness of his perspective and actions. At one point, I finally broke in and told Owen that I wasn't planning on reporting about my meeting with him, except "in therapy." He laughed and thanked me. Then he started to talk about his feelings, about his wife's (my secretary's) resignation, and he burst into tears. He talked some more, but the conversation had long since left the things he'd been hearing about me.

As immediately as he blustered in, Owen stood to leave. I asked him to sit back down. He did. I felt compelled for us to pray together and offer our conversation to God. He agreed, and after a brief silence we offered the conversation to God in our own way. He thanked me and left.

It feels like a victory. I felt powerful in that meeting.

How, in this account, did Larry demonstrate narrative leadership? First, he took a deep breath and realized that this meeting was going to take thoughtful preparation time. He gave himself that time. He quieted his anxiety by taking measures to keep from becoming Owen's next victim. He made phone calls to trusted people who could help him create a situation where Owen couldn't live out his familiar tale of intimidating the clergy. He summed up his leadership strategy when he said, *"Though the prevailing narrative is that Owen makes life harder, listen intently for the alternative story.*

Remain curious." He was aware that the story Owen brought in wasn't the only story about Owen. There were other narratives that disclosed his humanity. Larry took a curious, not-knowing position that waited to hear a clue to another story. He said further, *"This is not a time to explain, justify, or defend anything he brings to the table."* He knew Owen would expect him to do all these things, and *he decided in advance to take a non-defensive position.* Finally, he understood that Owen was his guest, and so it was Larry and not Owen who *had the prerogative to set a time limit on the visit.*

Larry's narrative leadership was both compassionate and firm. His consultation helped him change the usual story of *Owen the aggressor vs. the defending pastor.* His not-knowing approach placed Larry in a different position than others typically assumed with Owen. Setting aside the need for defense allowed him to listen to the deep need that Owen usually kept hidden beneath his exterior of hostility and judgment. Larry's curious attentiveness to this adversary's story opened up Owen's tears of sadness.

Narrative wisdom links curiosity and compassion. Owen's aggressiveness and belligerence usually prevented people from asking curious questions about him as a human being. He was disarmed when Larry asked with compassion and curiosity, "What do you want out of this conversation? What's motivating you to bring this to me now?"

The Calls Ministers Get

After Larry presented this case to his peer group, members began to wonder what *they* needed to ask themselves when they faced a situation where they were being challenged or asked to do something that they instinctively wanted to refuse. They came up with a list of twenty-three questions. The following questions from that long list stand out as guidance for narrative leadership:

These questions invigorate a leader's wisdom. They invite thoughtful reflection on an unfolding narrative and warn against plunging thoughtlessly into action. They bring into view the possibility of alternative narratives. When you read them you are reminded

QUESTIONS TO ASK WHEN PUT ON THE SPOT

Questions to get a clearer picture of the situation and to provide restraint from premature action:
- Am I about to rescue someone or some group when they need to handle the situation on their own?
- Am I being asked to cross a boundary I shouldn't? Are those making the request crossing a boundary they shouldn't?
- Must I respond now, or do I need to take time to think about it?

Questions to help manage the anxiety arising from the situation:
- Is it necessary to explain, justify, or defend myself in this situation?
- What am I afraid of, and what's the worst thing that could happen?

Questions that focus on key narratives:
- How can I take a not-knowing position and stay on the side of curiosity so I can get the full story?
- To what narrative am I giving the most power? Is this the only narrative? What are alternative narratives?

A question that speaks to isolation and loneliness:
- Who would I like to talk to about this situation? Who is trustworthy to keep this confidential and also is wise about such things?

that you need not be controlled by someone else's narrative. You can pay careful attention to it, explore it, and understand it, but you aren't obligated to adopt it as your story. It is possible that the other narrative will influence you and cause you to change your story, but that will be a conscious choice. You won't do it by default. Clergy in the project have posted these questions near their phone to ask themselves when they get a troublesome call. What questions would be useful to you to post by your phone?

The Surprise of Practice

"Questions to Ask When Put on the Spot" were questions produced by the group and were an invitation into *the practice of taking time to reflect before responding to demands*. These questions weren't imposed. They arose out of practices of the group over the five years of the project.

Practice flowed from the constant rhythm of participating in a group that adopted an unconventional narrative wisdom. Central to narrative wisdom is practicing the rule of "no fixing, no saving, no advising, no setting each other straight." This practice invited people into an unconventional conversation where *curiosity* and *not-knowing* led the way. Practice wasn't demanded of the participants; they were drawn into it, because it appealed to them. The participants taught us, the leaders, how practice was essential to the development of narrative leadership.

A useful metaphor for this practice is muscle memory. Whether it's dancing, playing the piano, driving a car, riding a bicycle, or cooking, muscles are trained deeply to do the activity so that people do it without thinking about it. (If you want to test the notion of muscle memory, try cooking in someone else's kitchen.) As we and the participants practiced narrative skills over time we began to change the "muscle memory" of certain patterns of thought and action.

Jim changed his strategy from staying ahead of the congregation to journeying with them. Gene walked away from putting up the vacation Bible school sign even though he felt the physical pull to do what he always did. Larry moved through his anxiety about Owen's visit by seeking consultation and giving this appointment far more prep time than normal. All of these actions challenged the conventional muscle memory that these clergy had developed in their theological education and years of pastoral ministry. These atypical actions grew out of practice. The regular practice of narrative thought and action began to change their typical ways of responding.

In this project the practice of narrative thinking and action was not a solitary undertaking. It was done in a community of people who were working together to find alternative ways of doing the work of ministry. The community provided a comradeship and a secure laboratory in which to practice this unconventional way of having a conversation.

We, the authors, do not respond to the word *practice* in the same way. Kelli says,

> I view practice in this project as a narrative about how different thought and behaviors arose within our clergy group unbidden, and how we thickened this unconventional narrative by sharing

stories of change. Most of my vocation has been in the context of the congregation or seminary staff. In both places there was always conversation about one more thing that clergy could do to become more effective. I became allergic to any advice or practice that promised to improve my work—the as-

> ### ALCOHOLICS ANONYMOUS
>
> Alcoholics Anonymous is an example of building cognitive and behavioral muscle memory. Against the heavy hand of addiction, people in AA band together to practice sobriety. They need each other to develop a new pattern that will sustain their sobriety—regular group meetings, telling personal narratives, companionship, pursuing the twelve steps, and living one day at a time.

sumption being my work was never good enough. On a personal level there is always potential for improvement, but the message of "practice" to ministers tends to be, "You are never good enough."

Dick says, "As a professor I witnessed the power of repetition and the deepening of skills by doing them again and again. I don't have the allergy that puts "practice" with "not good enough." Kelli responds,

> Due to my allergy, I emphasize that "practice" in this project was discovered, not imposed. No one was telling these clergy, "Here's what you need to do to improve your work." At the beginning of this project none of us knew that our narrative work together would become a rhythm and create a pattern for transformation. In short, I do not want to participate in one more thing that says, "This can improve your not-good-enough ministry." I want to bear witness to something that has been transformative for these clergy and offer it as a story to other clergy.

The place where Kelli and Dick do agree is that practice in this project was not imposed. Participants and leaders were drawn into it together.

As we began to recognize the "muscle" in these practices, we wondered how to identify the particular changes that were occurring in participants. One of them described this new "muscle memory" as a transformation—a change in outlook and action she was beginning to see in herself and her congregation. We turn, in the next chapter, to describe the signs of transformation we looked for in the ministers who had engaged in this practice. These signs would provide clues to tell us how the practice had affected their muscle memory of leadership.

CHAPTER 4 |

Signs of Transformation

Will accepted an invitation from his denomination to teach a brief course in pastoral counseling for ministers in a Central American country. He chose to use the narrative perspective of this project as his teaching approach. During his week of teaching he introduced the ministers to *the rule of "no fixing, no saving, no advising, no setting anyone straight."* He asked them to write down their earliest childhood memory and to relate it to a biblical story. He showed them how to find alternative narratives in their lives, and he demonstrated how to be curious and take a not-knowing position.

He told of his trip in a case presentation to his clergy peer group, asking Sally to be his conversation partner. He told about worship in that setting and about clapping and swaying with the people when the other Anglos held back. He sat by the roadside with a small group of local people after their car broke down. It was a pleasant afternoon, and as he sat there he realized he didn't need to be anywhere or do anything. "I didn't *care* that the car had broken down," he said. "No one at the church could reach me!" The conversation continued:

Will: This trip validated my own experience.

Sally: What was affirming to you?

Will: This approach is real countercultural. It was fun. I began to understand narrative better. It's scary! It's subversive to everything we've ever known. It's subversive to the church, to the nation! (Laughing) I might have been introducing a revolution!

Sally: What change is this going to make for you?

Will: Look at alternatives. There are other options. Ask "What are the alternatives?" There are layers and new chapters to write. I saw people being empowered by their story. Once we teach it, we're the ones that get booted out. This is their country, their story. I was walking around on sacred ground.

Sally: Does your concern about revolution in Central America apply to you and your congregation?

Will: Yes. Right now I have a board chair who wants it all laid out in the direction of a plan for church growth.

Sally: Is there some kind of longing you experienced there?

Will: There was a tension having to do with my lifestyle.

Sally: A longing for freedom?

Will: Yes. Why isn't that possible here?

The conversation shifted to include other group members.

Barbara: Would you like to be subversive?

Will: Yes, I was blacklisted by the Countrymen [the support group of denominational notables who invited Will to join and whom he turned down because they were all male, all white, and not open to homosexuals being members]. I've been blacklisted. You pay for being subversive.

Sally: We women are an alternative narrative by being senior pastors.

Kelli: As the first woman pastor in my congregation I had the freedom to rewrite the minister story.

Kelli: Why did you take this idea [of a narrative approach] to Central America?

Will: The old way isn't fun anymore.

Kelli: What was fun?

Will: Finding an alternative for my life.

Dick: What's the old story and the alternative?

Will: The old story is of my grandfather's suicide and my father's overdose on alcohol. I was stuck in that story. As I talked with my mentor, I looked at my mother's side of the family, which was different.

Will had used his time with his mentor in the project to rehearse with her the story of his life. He was already living a different life than his father and grandfather, but he had no place to retell this new narrative. In the safety of the mentoring relationship, he had the opportunity to look at the role models in his family of origin. He chose to look beyond the rather dramatic and overpowering stories of his father and grandfather to uncover the alternative narratives on his mother's side of the family. As he heard himself tell the alternative story he wanted to live out, he realized that in many ways he was already living it. Telling his story helped him recognize he was in the midst of a transformative experience. What happened to him in Central America was an expression of the transformation already going on in his life.

Telling one's story appears to be a simple thing. It is rare, however, for clergy to have the chance to tell an unedited story of their life to a listener who is genuinely curious and patient. Clergy are practiced at listening to the stories of congregants, but they seldom have the chance to narrate their own story. When they don't have a place to do this, they're less likely to have access to hidden narratives in their lives—hidden narratives that can tell of transformational possibilities.

Success or Transformation

Transformation refers to a change that affects everything we think and do. This change may be most evident in a change in world view, a change in character, a change in basic thinking, a change in attitude, or a change in one's course of action, to name a few. But each of these changes is a clue to a comprehensive change in one's life. Will's story offers evidence of transformation.

On our way to the idea of *transformation* we went first to *success*. How could we know whether our project was *successful*? That's quite a legitimate question to ask a project that's supported by grant funds. When we asked, What are the signs of success in this project? however, we came to question the idea of "success." It suggested a quantitative measure and an arrival at a goal. We recognized we were focused neither on quantitative results nor on achieving a goal. We wanted to know what happened when clergy knew their story and led with it. Did this have a transforming effect? Did it move them toward God's dream for humankind?

A Liminal Space

To set the table for transformational conversation among our participants we welcomed them into a space separated from their usual daily activity and secured by a covenant of confidentiality—a *liminal* space.

Here we offer a further consideration of liminality that we discussed briefly in chapter two. In his understanding of ritual, Victor Turner introduces two central ideas, *liminality* and *communitas*.[1] *Liminality* refers to a threshold situation where for a time people leave their ordinary worlds of roles, statuses, and familiar social structures. *Communitas* describes the quality of relationships in that liminal space. In liminal space people experience an immediacy in relationships, unmediated by status, role, or social conventions. In this state they are open to transformative change, because they are able to view their culture and themselves from a different perspective. *The basic rule of this project of "no fixing, no saving, no advising, no setting each other straight" expresses this communitas quality.* Persons in a liminal state have the freedom from role, status, and social expectations to explore their personal lives and to ask questions about their day-to-day life in the culture.

The liminality and communitas nurtured in our clergy groups invited transformation. Participants experienced a freedom from daily social transactions where they had to negotiate expectations demanded of their role and status. They entered into play and laughter. Turner says that in this state one is challenged to accept "the hard saying, 'except ye become as a little child.'"[2] That is the key to transformation.

Congregational worship may or may not open up the possibility for liminal experience in which transformation occurs. Retreats and mission trips can provide such possibilities. After a mission to a developing nation, people often return to the United States with a different purpose for their lives—one that's out of step with the culture of wealth and consumption. Rituals marking life transitions may lead people into a liminal state—the birth or baptism of a child, a bar or bat mitzvah, the marriage of a couple, the death of a family member.

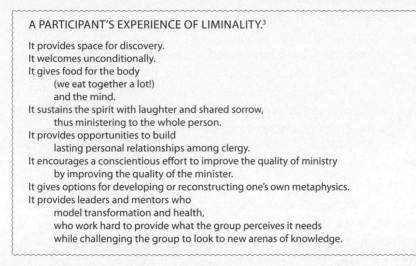

A PARTICIPANT'S EXPERIENCE OF LIMINALITY.[3]

It provides space for discovery.
It welcomes unconditionally.
It gives food for the body
    (we eat together a lot!)
    and the mind.
It sustains the spirit with laughter and shared sorrow,
    thus ministering to the whole person.
It provides opportunities to build
    lasting personal relationships among clergy.
It encourages a conscientious effort to improve the quality of ministry
    by improving the quality of the minister.
It gives options for developing or reconstructing one's own metaphysics.
It provides leaders and mentors who
    model transformation and health,
    who work hard to provide what the group perceives it needs
    while challenging the group to look to new arenas of knowledge.

Jesus's Dinner Table

In first-century Palestine, Jesus created liminal space by inviting people to an inclusive table fellowship. It was a space where they experienced a different kind of community—that suggested by Turner's idea of *communitas*. Jesus tells a parable of a great banquet in which a host's invitations are turned down repeatedly. The host then commands his servant, "Go out at once into the streets and lanes of the town and bring in the poor, the crippled, the blind, and the lame."[4] John Dominic Crossan describes the ensuing social situation: "If one actually brought in *anyone off the street*, one could, in such a situation, have classes, sexes, and ranks all mixed up together. Anyone could be reclining next to anyone else, female next to male, free next to slave, socially high next to socially low, and ritually pure next to ritually impure."[5] Crossan calls such a situation "open commensality." Commensality means "the rules of tabling and eating as miniature models for the rules of association and socialization."[6] This open commensality offered liminal space in which people related to each other in ways radically different from those dictated by the dominant social systems of Jerusalem and Rome.

Jesus's table practice was not something new. He was recovering an ancient Hebrew tradition. Prior to the monarchy in Israel, every meal was an occasion for a sacrifice. The sacrifice to God was woven together with eating and drinking. If there was a meal, it was an offering. If there was an offering, it was a meal. The meal in the presence of God established a covenant between God and the dinner guests and a covenant among the guests themselves.[7] When, in the establishment of the monarchy, worship and sacrifice were centralized at the temple in Jerusalem, worship was removed from its local environment. It lost its natural nourishment. A person "lived in Hebron, but sacrificed in Jerusalem; life and worship fell apart."[8]

In his table fellowship Jesus reunited worship and common meals. He created a liminal space for eating and drinking in the presence of God. He was calling people into a different kind of relationship than that prescribed by those in power. It was a taste of the messianic banquet—God's dream for humankind. And many emerged from these liminal experiences with a changed view of themselves, the world, and God. They emerged transformed. That liminal experience was the heartbeat of the early church—a community radically out of step with the centers of social power.

Six Signs of Transformation

With the help of the participants we developed a set of six signs of transformation, which we've written in the form of questions. These questions are reference points that helped us find clues to transformative experiences. The transformative experiences we describe here are rooted in a participant's entire life; they are not necessarily an "outcome" of this project. From participant narratives, however, we are able to gain a clearer picture of the relationship between narrative leadership and transformation. The questions are:

1. *How do clergy view their work through the lens of covenant?*
2. *How do they define themselves and stay connected to those who disagree with them?*
3. *How do they advocate for justice?*
4. *How do they observe Sabbath?*
5. *How do they find ongoing community with clergy peers?*
6. *How do they express and invite playfulness?*

1. How Do Clergy View Their Work through the Lens of Covenant?

Kay was associate pastor at a large, prosperous, multi-staff congregation. She was responsible for the church's mission ministry and was successful at it. She was well prepared for this role, her seminary doctoral project having been a study of homelessness in a large southern city. Her success won the hearts of many in the congregation. After a time the senior minister told her he thought she needed to lead a congregation of her own and that she should be looking for another appointment. Kay was newly divorced and working hard to care for two teenage daughters. She wanted to remain in the same city as her ex-husband in order for the children to have equal access to both parents. She was determined not to move away, and she resisted the senior minister's efforts to dismiss her. His efforts included recruiting people close to her to tell her it was time for her to find another position.

Things came to a critical point in her annual performance review with the pastor, the chair of the personnel committee, and three other leaders. She was asked whether she had made progress in finding another position. She answered that she thought it inappropriate for her to discuss that subject in her annual review, "but I'll talk about it anyway," she said. "I think it would be irresponsible for me to move out of the area." In the course of the review, the chair of the personnel committee, who was supportive of her, asked if she would like to talk with him on a more regular basis. She said, "It would be much better than having different people sent to check up on me." She didn't rescue the group from awkward silences. Throughout she was gracious, and the pastor commented, "You keep being gracious." She called attention to the fact that she was ultimately accountable to the denominational judicatory that held the power to hire and dismiss. Worried, the pastor said, "Are you going to bring charges?" The power in the room had shifted. When she described this situation to her clergy group, she said it was a *kairos* moment for her, with significance far beyond her relationship with the senior minister. She was practicing a new narrative of gracious assertiveness, refusing to give in to the will of a powerful male. She said, "It was Dragon: zero, and Princess: two."

Kay said no to the senior pastor's wishes and *yes to the covenant that defined her role and status as an associate minister to the congregation*. This covenant was spelled out in the policies of her denomination and sustained by the local denominational judicatory. A promise had been made, and acting against the superior power of the senior minister, she held to it. Ultimately she did leave this position, but she did so on her own terms after negotiating a call as senior minister to a congregation in another city.

COVENANT AND THE EXODUS STORY

Covenants are imbedded in narratives. Kay's covenant with the pastor and the congregation is explored and understood through narrative—hers, the senior minister's, the personnel committee's, and the narratives of people beyond that circle. Israel's formational covenant, the Decalogue, is imbedded in the Exodus narrative, succinctly told in the first commandment. "I am the LORD your God, who brought you out of the land of Egypt, out of the house of slavery; you shall have no other gods before me."[9]

Separated from the Exodus narrative, the Decalogue is a set of abstract rules. Without the narrative, its life blood is drained away. Within the narrative of liberation from Egypt, the Decalogue is an expression of God's grace and provision for a community where people are oriented toward a just and compassionate deity, where they respect and protect the rights of the weakest members, and where they can live without fear.

The real miracle of the Exodus is neither in the plagues that fell on Egypt nor in the escape through the sea. It is the establishment of a covenantal community in which the distinctions of peasant and ruling classes—a distinction that prevailed in every society at that time—are replaced by an egalitarian system of community promises that is without parallel in the ancient world. Walter Brueggemann describes the Decalogue as the foundation for "a radical reordering of social relations" that departs from the stratification and abuse in the peasant culture of Egypt. This egalitarian covenant "unleash[ed] in the world a genuine alternative to hierarchical, stratified monopoly." The Exodus story and the covenant at Sinai are touchstones for the prophets, who challenged Israel's monarchy for reestablishing a peasant society that put most of the population back into servitude. The Exodus society is at the root of all theories of democratic society. "Moses at Sinai thus states a deep either/or. When one embraces Yahweh, one embraces not only a very different God, but also membership in a very different social practice."[10]

Narrative clergy leadership has theological roots in the story of the Exodus covenant and in Jesus, whose mission was to restore that covenant of equality. He welcomed the poor and the outcast. He extended the covenant of the kingdom of God—God's dream—to those without power. A covenant of equality subverts attempts at social domination and exploitation, and it gives rise to leadership that is more invitational than coercive, more equalitarian than hierarchical, more communal than stratified. Such leadership maintains curiosity, listens to stories told and for those not being told, and helps others use their own wisdom rather than telling them what to do.

COVENANT AND THE CONGREGATION

This covenantal vision leads clergy to pay attention to congregational processes. They think about *how tasks are accomplished* within the congregation. They see their job as stewards of the covenant, and they keep focused on the process. It's not their job to guarantee a particular outcome. They ask questions such as: Is the decision-making process clear to everyone? Are we rushing to a decision without giving people time to reflect on it? Are people who have a stake in the outcome participating in the decision? Are minority views given voice and respected? Do we need outside consultation? The minister doesn't presume to know in advance how to tackle the problem or opportunity and pays as much attention to the process as to the issue itself.

ASSUMPTIVE COVENANTS[11]

Most of the covenants that clergy negotiate are not explicit ones but are implied; they are assumed. And an assumptive covenant is usually not apparent until someone thinks it's been broken.

The setting was a Wednesday evening Bible study. One of our participants, an associate pastor, led it. A husband and wife dominated the conversation with their questions and arguments. Few others had a chance to speak. The associate tried with little success to steer the dialogue constructively. Quitting time approached, and the couple forged on with no regard for the clock. Then a woman who was a respected, long-time member, stood up, said that it was time to go, and dismissed the meeting! The associate was stunned and hurt by her abrupt action. He felt rebuked and diminished. Days later he was with the woman and asked, "What was going on the other night in the Bible study?" She told him that the couple had dominated the Bible study in the past and regularly pushed it into overtime. She finally was fed up with it and decided to stop the meeting. She did not mean her action as a rebuke to the associate; she thought she was helping him. The associate was relieved to hear that her action was aimed at the couple and not at him.

As he and the clergy group reflected on this event, they identified the several assumptive covenants at work. The woman who called an end to the meeting assumed a covenant that church meetings would end on time. This was reinforced by the fact that she had suffered under a former pastor who regularly preached beyond noon, violating the assumptive covenant that Sunday morning worship ends at twelve. The dominating couple assumed a covenant that said that no matter what time it was, they could claim the floor until their views prevailed. The associate assumed that his presentation would be heard, that a polite discussion would follow, and that it was his job to bring the meeting to a close. It was a set-up for misunderstanding, as assumptive covenants collided with each other.

Pastoral leadership takes place in a web of assumptive covenants—sets of promises that are not spelled out and agreed to and that usually lie outside people's awareness. Often these assumptive covenants serve a constructive purpose—parishioners being able to count on the pastor's presence in times of suffering and grief, people acting to protect the privacy of the pastor and her family, church school teachers showing up faithfully, the finance committee managing the church's business in a responsible manner, people bringing food when someone is ill or has died.

Assumptive covenants, however, can also be a great source of confusion and difficulty, as people set out on a task with certain expectations only to discover that they are at cross purposes with others. Narrative leadership is curious about the presence of assumptive covenants. The most remarkable part of the associate pastor's story is that he asked the woman who had hurt him (by ending the meeting) what precipitated her action. That one question uncovered a web of assumptive covenants, and he discovered that she supported him after all.

ASSUMPTIVE COVENANTS ABOUT CONFIDENTIALITY

When the issue of confidentiality comes up in a group, assumptive covenants are attached to responses such as these:

- One person says, "I'm sure we all agree to treat this conversation confidentially." No one responds, but the speaker assumes agreement.
- "Can we all agree that we will keep what goes on in this group here and not share it with others?" Everyone nods consent.
- "I'm going to tell you something, but you must promise not to tell anyone else." The listener nods.
- "For this group to develop trust, we all must promise to keep strictly confidential what we say here. Can we agree to that?" The speaker gets consent from every person.

In each of these approaches the *meaning* of the promise of confidentiality is not addressed. There is no collective understanding of it. If there are ten people in the group, there may be ten different understandings of what confidentiality means. The promises above pull in their wake clusters of assumptive covenants.

PRACTICING COVENANTS OF CONFIDENTIALITY

In our clergy groups, confidentiality was our most important covenant. As project leaders we made a written proposal to the group for a covenant of confidentiality. Group members offered ideas for modifying our proposal. We came to agreement on a covenant that everyone could support. The covenant stated that no one in the group could share the stories of another group member without that member's explicit permission. It required that the project leaders ask permission to use a group member's information in research, publication, or public presentations. In such cases the identity of the group member and the member's congregation would be thoroughly disguised. In one group the participants, having received the promise that their material would be changed to protect their identity, gave the leaders general permission to use their stories in research, publication, and presentations. Another group required that the leaders get permission each time they used any member's personal story.

2. How Do Clergy Define Themselves and Stay Connected to Those Who Disagree with Them?

Covenant and self-definition are reciprocal signs of transformation. People cannot enter into a covenant without defining themselves. Covenanting requires they take a stand to say, "I choose to abide by this promise. These are my values. This is who I am." When called on to make a covenant, persons have to consider, "Who am I to make such a promise? Are these my values? Am I willing to stand by this commitment?" When covenants are broken, it may be the result of a failure of self-definition.

The idea of self-definition and self-differentiation originated in Bowen family systems theory[12]; then it was adopted by Rabbi Edwin Friedman as a key to effective leadership in churches and synagogues. *Self-definition* describes how a leader states her position without trying to coerce others to accept it. Kay, for example, from the story at the beginning of the previous section, takes an "I" position about what she's willing and not willing to do. She does not condemn the senior pastor's view, and she doesn't complain that he's being unfair. The term *self-differentiation* puts the focus on the leader's intention to stay connected as a separate self with those who disagree with her. Kay doesn't try to avoid the senior pastor. She stands toe-to-toe with him as she defines herself.

LEADING THROUGH SELF-DEFINITION AND SELF-DIFFERENTIATION

The basic concept of leadership through self-differentiation is this: If a leader will take primary responsibility for his or her own position as "head" and work to define his or her own goals and self, while *staying in touch* with the rest of the organism, there is a more than reasonable chance that the body will follow. There may be initial resistance but, if the leader can stay in touch with the resisters, the body will usually go along. This emphasis on the leader's self-differentiation is not to be confused with independence or some kind of selfish individuality. On the contrary, we are talking here about the ability of a leader to be a self while still remaining a part of the system.[13]

—EDWIN FRIEDMAN

As the senior minister pressed Kay to find another position, *she consistently defined herself*—saying what she could and could not do, according to her own priorities (such as her children). She had seen how the senior minister intimidated and extracted resignation letters from other female staff members he no longer wanted to work with—actions that congregational leaders had not resisted. She was determined she would not be his next victim. Although she knew her days as a minister in that congregation were numbered, she was going to follow her own wisdom and not be pressured into decisions that were not in her best interest.

Transformation occurred, not so much in Kay's defeat of the senior minister, but in her ability to define herself. Her capacity to do this was evident in her self-definition in other arenas. For example, she became more self-defined with her ex-husband and asserted herself to gain custody of her children.

3. How Do Clergy Advocate for Justice?

Covenants are closely linked to justice. The Exodus covenant protected people from abuse and exploitation. It prevented the strong from taking advantage of the weak. It created safety for everyone and made possible an egalitarian community. When the monarchy was established, the royal house of Israel reinstituted a society where the ruling class made their wealth on the backs of peasant farmers. The Exodus covenant was dismantled. The Hebrew prophets condemned this system of exploitation and pressed for social justice to be restored.

Jesus acted out of this prophetic tradition as an advocate for the oppressed. In the synagogue at Nazareth he linked his work of justice to the prophet Isaiah: "The Spirit of the Lord is upon me, because he has anointed me to bring good news to the poor. He has sent me to proclaim release to the captives and recovery of sight to the blind, to let the oppressed go free, to proclaim the year of the Lord's favor." He then said, "Today this scripture has been fulfilled in your hearing."[14] He was restoring the Exodus covenant of justice.

In the course of this project, Sadie took a position as Minister to the University at a denominational school. The school attracted a mixed student body of African-American and white students. Sadie set about to minister to all the students as a community of equals, but she encountered the unspoken dominant narrative of an institution that saw itself as a place of traditional, southern, white Christianity. Sadie led with curiosity about an unequal social covenant. She wanted to know why time-worn practices of racial discrimination should be perpetuated at the school. Her ministry helped promote a different narrative—one in which African-American students got from her equal treatment and equal press as representatives of the school. Among her several initiatives to develop a practice of equality, she encouraged an African-American student gospel choir. She helped them get venues for performance in the area. The choir's high level of participation and its success as an expression of the vitality of the school began to tip the scales toward racial social justice on campus. Using narrative wisdom, instead of fighting directly against the discrimination, she found a way to thicken the narrative of the gifts and vitality of African-American students. As this narrative grew stronger, the discrimination narrative was weakened.

THE LANGUAGE OF INJUSTICE

A narrative perspective leads inevitably to questions of justice, because it asks questions about language and how language shapes what we see to be reality. Language is used to create and perpetuate unjust social arrangements. Barbara, a co-pastor with her husband, sang in the church choir. The choir director presented a hymn for the upcoming service that used the phrase "brother man," among other non-inclusive language choices. Barbara asked the choir, "Do we want to sing a hymn that leaves out half of the congregation?" She didn't let the hymn choice go by without notice. Thereby she awakened curiosity about the way masculine metaphors and pronouns exclude women. As she told this story in her clergy peer group, she said that her comment hadn't made any difference. It is important to note, however, that from a narrative perspective the introduction of even a small justice question will not be lost. Barbara understood the power of language to define reality, to communicate "this is the way the world is." And she knew that a phrase like "brother man" was unjust because it fed cultural narratives that regarded women as lesser beings than men.

Barbara's question resonates with the work of Paulo Freire, a Brazilian educator who in the 1950s became a success at teaching rural and urban peasants how to read. He led interdisciplinary teams to live with the peasants and to learn their idiom. How did they talk with each other about the things most important to them? What were their habits of speech? Educators gathered small circles of peasants to learn these things. They showed them pictures and listened carefully to their responses. They then built their literacy exercises on the peasant idiom. An analogy to Barbara's intervention would be to ask women how they would write hymns if they weren't influenced by patriarchal conventions.

In Freire's project, one group of tenement residents was shown a picture of a drunken man walking on the street and three young men conversing on the corner. The investigator was surprised to hear the group say, "The only one there who is productive and useful to his country is the souse who is returning home after working all day for low wages and who is worried about his family because he can't take care of their needs. He is the only worker. He is a decent worker and a souse like us." The investigator had intended to study their attitudes toward alcoholism. Instead he heard them make the connection between low wages, feeling exploited, being unable to support their family, and getting drunk. They identified with the drunkard—he was them; this was their predicament.[15] With this kind of information the literacy program could teach these workers how to read using their own narratives, narratives that were different from the dominant narratives of the ruling class. The literacy program could use narratives that understood the root causes of alcohol abuse, and this was quite different from the moralizing about alcohol abuse the workers heard from the dominant culture.

Freire confessed that he was at first naïve about the political implications of his literacy work. After a political coup destroyed his project and put him in prison, however, he no longer underestimated the threat that such education posed to a government that intended to keep peasants in their place.

And if anyone doubts the risks involved in Barbara's question, let them talk to clergy who have introduced inclusive language in hymns and scripture in the worship service.

LITTLE NARRATIVES OF HOPE

As we have seen, a major theme in narrative work is the belief that *there's always more than one story* about an event, a social arrangement, a person's life. When people see there's an alternative narrative, they then can compare it to the most visible story to see which one is more just, more faithful to God's dream. Kelli says, "If I am looking at a piece of clothing and can't tell whether it's black or midnight blue, I can get another item that I know to be midnight blue and compare them. Then I can tell for sure. Yes, it's black. But I can't really tell until I have the two pieces together. Alternative narratives help you gain clarity. Sometimes the only way to identify a dominant narrative is by finding a little narrative that's different."

A narrative understanding of social justice does not despair in the face of grand narratives of oppression. *It values little narratives of hope and change against grand narratives that protect the status quo.* Dorothea, a participant who was pastor of a predominantly lesbian and gay congregation, decided to use St. Benedict's *lectio divina*—the meditative practice we employed at the beginning of each of our group sessions—in a morning worship service in which she preached a sermon, "Being Who God Created You to Be." She used a text from Psalm 139: "It was you who formed my inward parts; you knit me together in my mother's womb. I praise you, for I am fearfully and wonderfully made."[16] She read it three times and allowed for a period of silence between the readings. She reported that with the third reading, "I had them interject their name, and then I just let it sit for a while. The response was this intense silence with the sound of sobbing mixed in." It was a little narrative telling that God created and blessed them, told against a grand narrative that said God rejected them. It was a simple but profound act of social justice.

4. How Do Clergy Observe Sabbath?

As we explored the meaning of sabbath in one group, and discussed whether we all practiced it, we decided to ask, Is meeting here in this project group a sabbath for you? This prompted the following conversation:

Gene: It's the only sabbath I have! For five years this has given me a regular sabbath.

Sandra: Now that I have to travel a long distance to come to the group, it gives me two days to be on sabbath.

Sally: I don't know if this fits what I understand to be sabbath. This is about me and not about God.

Jim: Keeping sabbath is a spiritual discipline. I've got to put this sermon down and go to this group. It's a discipline of the spirit to do so.

Kathy: Sabbath is a time to be rather than to do. Here we wrestle with a lot.

Sally: I love this time. It draws me close to God. But it's not rest.

Sandra: But it's a break from our normal routine.

Gene: Maybe a better word is *respite* rather than sabbath.

Jim: I can celebrate sabbath by myself. This community is the only place I come where I don't feel judged.

Kelli: How can we have sabbath as a sign of transformation in this culture?

Jim: How do we model sabbath for the people?

Kathy: As a minister I work on Sabbath. I can have times of sabbath during the week, but it's not enough.

In this conversation there is debate not only about whether the group time is sabbath but what sabbath is, period. Participants identify *elements* of sabbath in their time together: It separates them from their work routine. No one is judging anyone else. Some have depended on it as their main place of sabbath. Others hold back from calling it sabbath because it involves the hard work of exploring and understanding their story and their leadership.

So, what is sabbath? Sabbath, like justice, is imbedded in God's covenant with Israel. It is the fourth commandment, depending on how you count them. In the book of Exodus the sabbath command is warranted because God rested on the seventh day of creation: "For in six days the LORD made heaven and earth, the sea, and all that is in them, but rested the seventh day; therefore the LORD blessed the sabbath day and consecrated it."[17] In Deuteronomy the command is warranted by the exodus from Egypt: "Remember that you were a slave in the land of Egypt, and the LORD your God brought you out from there with a mighty hand and an outstretched arm; therefore the LORD your God commanded you to keep the sabbath day."[18]

The sabbath command in Deuteronomy looks backward to Pharaoh's relentless productivity where there was toil without rest. In Exodus the command looks forward to the restoration of God's intent in creation. The command is "an enactment of peaceableness" where people are engaged "in a neighbor-respecting life that is not madly engaged in production and consumption."[19]

It may be that no other commandment is more difficult to translate into our culture than sabbath observance. Translating sabbath from an ancient agrarian culture into a diverse postmodern one is complicated. While sabbath is essential, and clergy know this, it is important to honor the complexity of what seems to be a simple command to rest. How could a command to rest be so challenging?

Our clergy participants were in a hurry. They had long to-do lists, and they were pursued by guilt that told them, "You're not doing enough!" They led congregations that were saturated in expectations of production and progress. Wayne Muller in his book on sabbath says these expectations are created by the *eschatology* of contemporary Western society: "We call our particular messianic eschatology *progress*. . . . We are on the glory road, we are hurtling toward the *eschaton*. . . . We never rest on our laurels, we never rest at all. Every moment is a necessary investment in the divinely ordained and completely unquestioned goal of progress." Sabbath challenges this theology of progress, says Muller, by calling us to stop and take in the blessed present. He writes, "The gifts of grace and delight are present and abundant; the time to live and love and give thanks and rest and delight is now. . . . We do not have miles to go before we sleep. The time to sleep, to rest, is now."[20]

For our participants, and for us, obedience to the sabbath command is a work in progress. The command to rest, as Muller says, goes against the relentless and idolatrous quest to reach the false eschaton of progress. The fourth commandment is a barrier against the idolatry stated in the first commandment, "I am the LORD your God, who brought you out of the land of Egypt, out of the house of slavery; you shall have no other gods before me."[21] To rest every seventh day is a barrier to idolatry because it stops us in our tracks in our idolatrous quest. Sabbath says a decisive no to this relentless effort.

We found only small narrative fragments that showed that we or the participants had made sabbath a part of the rhythm of our lives. Yet the dialogue above provides evidence that some participants experienced sabbath time in their clergy peer group meetings. When clergy entered their groups, there were times they experienced sabbath rest. We would say they *tasted* sabbath. They did not get a full meal of it, but they tasted it.

5. How Do Clergy Find Ongoing Community with Clergy Peers?

Between the exodus from Egypt and the delivery of the Decalogue, Moses faces an organizational crisis. He spends all day every day handling questions and disputes while people stand around him to have their turn. His father-in-law Jethro comes to visit him and observes this situation. He asks Moses, "What is this that you are doing for the people? Why do you sit alone, while all the people stand around you from morning until evening?"[22] Moses explains, "Because the people come to me to inquire of God. When they have a dispute, they come to me and I decide between one person and another, and I make known to them the statutes and instructions of God." Jethro says, "What you are doing is not good. You will surely wear yourself out, both you and these people with you. For the task is too heavy for you; you cannot do it alone." Then Jethro tells Moses how to enlist and organize others to share his leadership burden. Moses realizes his predicament and takes Jethro's advice. Notice Jethro's key phrases:

> Why do you sit alone?
> You will surely wear yourself out
>   for the task is too heavy for you.
> You cannot do it alone.
> Look for able people.
> They will bear the burden with you.
> Then you will be able to endure.

It doesn't take much imagination to see here a description of overburdened, lonely ministers. This narrative is a formula for relief and a cautionary tale for survival. Clergy need a community of their own in order "to be able to endure." What kind of group will give this support?

A PEER GROUP OUTSIDE THE CONGREGATION AND DENOMINATION

Kathy observed, "As clergy we work hard to create a community we can never be part of." Ministers are a part of their congregations, yes, but the congregation, or groups in it, can't serve effectively as their peer group. For one thing, other clergy "get it." Sally had recently come to the church as its senior minister. She was called to provide pastoral care to a family in the church. It was not long before she discovered that a former pastor was also seeing the family.

His intervention was clearly against the policy of the denomination. She contacted him in an attempt to set clearer boundaries and found him difficult to deal with. She told this story to her clergy peer group. They immediately understood why she was troubled by the former pastor's behavior. She reported, "I told my husband about this, and he didn't see the problem. He thought I should be happy to have help with the situation. He didn't get it," she said, "but *you* get it!"

In this project we found that whatever their denomination, clergy peers generally understood the issues and problems of their minister companions. They had an inside track to comprehend the isolation, the chaos, the endless demands, and the conflicts that go with clergy leadership. Participants expressed relief to be able to tell their stories and know that the other clergy in the group "get it."

DIVERSITY VERSUS COMPETITION

In this project, clergy groups were made up of persons from different faith groups. Participants told us often that this diversity created the possibility for intimacy and self-disclosure that would not have been possible if all the group members were from the same denomination. The diversity lowered the competition that can infect clergy groups of the same denomination. As Sadie put it, "The egos got checked at the door. We were a very strong group with healthy egos, but we never did the traditional ministerial bragging about numbers or budgets, and I never felt anyone jockeyed for positions of power. It was very liberating."

EMPOWERING SELF-DEFINITION

A peer group of other clergy can provide support for self-definition, as it did for Sandra, who had been pastor for a year and a half at a congregation in a growing community. The church had a debt of more than a million dollars on its new sanctuary, and it needed to retire this debt before building new educational space. The finance committee considered the challenge and voted five to four to recommend to the church council a capital campaign to retire the debt. Sandra knew better than to trust such a split vote, but how would she take the lead to draw people toward a more solid decision?

The day after this vote her clergy group discussed "making sustainable decisions." One of the methods discussed was a gradient of agreement scale,[23] which gives group members a way to weigh their support for a decision on an eight-point scale. "That's exactly what I needed last night!" she said. With this idea of helping each person interpret where she or he stood, she was able to define herself more clearly and to know what to do next. She called a meeting with the chairs of the finance committee and the church council, discussed the problem of the weak vote, introduced the gradient of agreement scale, and said she would like to see a joint meeting of the two groups. The chairs supported this and called a joint meeting. She ended up not using the gradient. Instead she asked each person to express his or her view. At the end of this process everyone supported the decision. Her clergy peer group provided Sandra with an alternative narrative about making the decision and supported her as she defined herself clearly to the finance committee and church council.

Every day a wide variety of congregational expectations flows toward ministers. People with differing ideas about the pastor's role call on the phone, send e-mail, and drop by to express themselves. Many of these expectations involve taking charge to fix things that are awry—things that often are entirely outside the minister's job. Then there is the underground flow of internal expectations made up of what ministers *believe* people expect—whether they do or not. Our clergy groups gave participants a place to reflect on the flow of expectations coming toward them. Peers helped them define or redefine themselves and stick to it. The peer groups lowered anxiety and helped create a balance between external (and internal) expectations and the minister's understanding of her or his covenant with God and the congregation.

A COVENANT OF CONFIDENTIALITY

In the earlier discussion of covenant, the first sign of transformation, we described how promises of confidentiality are essential to provide the security and intimacy necessary for a clergy peer group. Even a group of trustworthy people with good intentions will only go so far in sharing their vulnerabilities unless everyone is committed to a clearly-stated covenant of confidentiality.

In their congregations, clergy edit what they say. They can't afford the risk to say many of the things on their minds. Nor should they do so. The promise of confidentiality in the project groups, and the developing trust, gave participants greater freedom to speak frankly without heavily editing their words.

Sadie, who is single, told how a member of her congregation, someone she thought understood her, gave her a "Mr. Wonderful" doll. When you pressed his stomach he said such things as, "I'd like to do the dishes," "Here, you take the remote," and "I'll clean the house." It was clear the woman did *not* understand, and Sadie was angry. Later that evening she heard the doll voicing these platitudes from the other room. She discovered that her dog had pulled the doll off the table and was punching its stomach with her nose. Then the dog proceeded to tear its head off. Sadie could hardly stop laughing. She told this story to her group, and group members began to make up statements for a doll named "Clergy Wonderful"—"I'll be glad to make a hospital visit to see your aunt's sister-in-law's brother's niece," "Please feel free to use the parsonage stove to cook the Thanksgiving turkey," "Of course I can perform your Christmas Eve wedding," and so forth. This theme was played out in the group for months. Where else could it happen?

INVESTING TIME AND ENERGY IN A PEER GROUP

The transformative experiences we have seen in this project were made possible mainly through the clergy peer groups. The groups provided the energy, the personal support, the chance to share pain and joy, the collective wisdom, and the accountability for participants to lead with self-definition and courage.

We have seen the transformative power that comes out of these groups. But can ministers organize and sustain a peer group based on narrative theory and supportive of narrative clergy leadership—and do it without the financial resources of a grant and full-time facilitators? This book is our attempt to address the question. The book tells the story of the project—a story told mainly by the participants. It provides a narrative that you as a reader may join.

6. *How Do Clergy Express and Invite Playfulness?*

"Humor and playfulness have infected my thinking," tells one of our participants,

> particularly in areas of church life that have become encumbered by an assumed solemnity. Where is the fun in the budget? Can you laugh in worship? Can the pastor make mistakes? Can we find some way to enjoy or appreciate our time together? It is not as simple as "laughter being the best medicine." There is an art to good playfulness. It is important to pick your spots. Playful interaction within the congregation, however, inoculates against the infectious tendency of conventional wisdom to assume that the worship and service of God calls us to remove ourselves from the joy of living. Laughter also destabilizes the tendency of the solemn or serious matters of church business to dominate or control the whimsical wind of God's Spirit blowing through the congregation.

Playfulness emerges in collegial community and is a clue that transformation is in the air. This playfulness is not toxic and does not carry an edge of competition or hostility. We have seen participants escape from the burdens of their work as they laugh at themselves, tell hilarious stories of life in their congregations, play practical jokes, subvert their leaders, and generally let their hair down. Playfulness can express a spiritual freedom—freedom from attachments to outcomes, from willfully pushing parishioners somewhere. Deadly over-seriousness is relieved because we understand that this ministry is primarily about God, not us. Playfulness can be a sign that we are giving up the demand to know, to be the expert, the rescuer, and trust God for the outcome.

This occurred in the first meeting of one clergy group: Dick left the group briefly and in the few moments he was away someone said, "Let's all change seats!" Immediately everyone made the move. Dick returned, looked puzzled, and said, "What's going on here?" Quite unexpectedly he had been pulled into play. He laughed. Everyone laughed at the wildness of a playful idea and its enactment in a matter of seconds. Their collective wisdom told them it was time to play.

The Old Testament speaks of play in the form of dance: "Then the prophet Miriam, Aaron's sister, took a tambourine in her hand; and all the women went out after her with tambourines and with dancing."[24] We hear that "David danced before the LORD with all his might."[25] Describing the walk of faith as a dance, the hymn proclaims, "Dance, then, wherever you may be, for I am the Lord of the Dance, said he." Most ministers have few places to play and enjoy the dance. In our clergy groups, they created a space to dance and play.

Edwin Friedman talks about play versus seriousness. "Seriousness is more than an attitude," he says, "it is a total orientation, a way of thinking embedded in constant, chronic anxiety. It is characterized by lack of flexibility in response, a narrow repertoire of approaches, persistent efforts to try harder, an inability to change direction, and a loss of perspective and concentrated focus." He says play is the antidote to the seriousness-anxiety syndrome. Playfulness is not a matter of joking or one-liners. It expresses a different orientation toward the world. "When playfulness is introduced into a 'serious' relationship system, family or congregation, it can break the vicious feedback cycle that is keeping a problem chronic."[26]

Clues in the Landscape

These six signs of transformation are broad landscapes of clergy thought and practice. Within these landscapes, in the stories of our participants, we found clues to transformative experiences.

Kay *honored the covenant* that maintained her position as associate pastor. The clue to her faithfulness to that covenant was her ability to say no when the senior minister attempted to force her resignation. When a woman closed down the Bible study session led by her new associate minister, he didn't retreat from her but rather followed his curiosity to ask her what happened at that meeting. This was a clue to his sensitivity to covenants. The conversation that followed revealed the cluster of assumptive covenants at work in that meeting. In both these situations a clue to transformation lay in *the ministers' ability to define themselves*—one by standing firm with a covenant and the other by inquiring just what the covenants might be.

Sadie, Minister to the University, expressed *the transformative sign of justice* with African American students by helping them create a gospel choir. Her clue to transformation came in her thickening the story of the gifts and vitality of these marginalized students. As Barbara's church choir set about to rehearse a hymn full of exclusively-male language, she asked, "Do we want to sing a hymn that leaves out half of the congregation?" Her awareness was a clue of her ability to see a social justice issue where others could not.

Another justice clue came from Dorothea, pastor of a lesbian and gay congregation. She took an ancient ritual, the *lectio divina* of St. Benedict, and used it to convey to a congregation of people wounded by social prejudice the good news that they were "fearfully and wonderfully made" by a God who cherished them.

Project participants pondered the question, Is meeting here in this project group a sabbath for you? It led them into a thick discussion of their *ambivalence about sabbath practice* and the ambiguities surrounding a clergy person's attempts to practice sabbath. The transformative clue in this conversation was their honest struggle with the wide gap between their belief in sabbath and how difficult it is to practice it.

Sally's statement to her group, "*You* get it!" expresses the vital place of a *clergy peer group* for sustaining ministers. A transformative clue emerged from within the diversity of the group, which contributed to the lowering of competition and the increase of trust. Another transformative clue came from the fact that the participants kept showing up. They invested their time and money and stayed in the groups for two years, and then some continued beyond those original groups for one or two years more.

"Let's all change seats!" set the beginning tone for one group when they switched chairs in the few seconds Dick was out of the room. It was a clue that these *serious ministers were ready to play.*

How have these signs of transformation been sustained over time—and how can you sustain them in your life? How have they been played out in the life of the congregations these ministers serve—and how can you play them out in yours? In the next chapter we explore these questions.

CHAPTER 5

Leading the Congregation with Your Story

Barbara tells the story of a member of her congregation giving her an American flag "to be displayed on the right hand of the altar." Her clergy peer group, she recalled, "had a field day with humorous places and uses for the flag—other than the designated one." "Not to be unpatriotic," she said, but "I feel the flag is second to God in our worship space and is better displayed elsewhere. The group's fun led me to think outside the box. Eventually this was handled well and the pastors were not labeled 'anti-flag' as some had hoped we would be. The donation lives in our entry space to remind us that American freedom of religion guarantees our entry into worship."

Barbara faced the delicate and risky business of finding a way to maintain a separation between the worship of God and a patriotic display of the flag. She knew there were some in the congregation lying in wait to see if they might label her and her co-pastor husband "anti-flag." Bringing the story to her clergy peer group helped her steer her way through this narrow strait. She was aware of the powerful patriotism narrative in the culture and in the congregation. And she believed that the worship of God would be compromised by the presence of the national flag at the altar. The playful response of her clergy peer group helped to lower her anxiety and "to think outside the box." In the process she developed *an alternative narrative* that said the flag stands for our country's guarantee of the freedom of religion. Playfulness opened up the landscape to find an alternative narrative that both honored the gift of the flag and placed it outside the worship space.

This narrative contains three primary themes: (1) *a clergy peer group* where Barbara could take her problem—how to respond to a strings-attached gift; (2) *the theological issue* at the heart of the story—keeping the worship of God separate from patriotism; and (3) *an act of narrative leadership*—crafting an alternative narrative that turned the situation on its head, causing the flag to symbolize the protection of freedom of religion. Following the themes in this story, in this chapter we tell what we learned about:

- The reciprocal relationship between participation in a clergy peer group and narrative congregational leadership.
- The changes in theological outlook that occurred in this relationship.
- How narrative leadership can bring about changes in a congregation's culture.

The Reciprocal Relationship between the Clergy Peer Groups and Congregational Leadership

Participation in these clergy peer groups, where members practiced a narrative perspective, began to affect the way they led their congregations. As we examined the stories of these ministers, we saw a reciprocal relationship between their congregational leadership and their participation in their clergy peer groups.

They Were Stuck in an Old Story of Disappointment

"Many times pastors and congregations feel that they are 'stuck' with the direction or circumstances of their present narrative," Ben writes.

Here's the story: For more than twelve years the building next door to the church sat empty. The owners of the property vacated it at that time because the church leadership told them they were "interested in purchasing the property as soon as it was

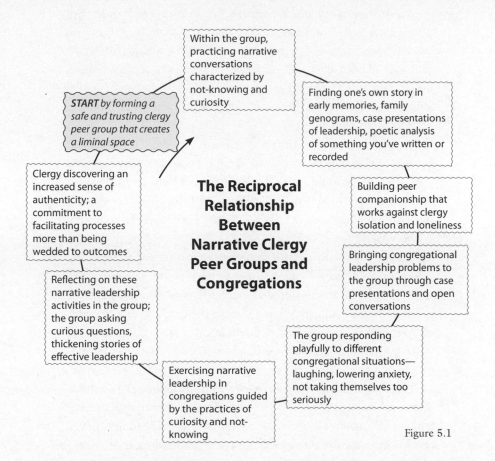

The Reciprocal Relationship Between Narrative Clergy Peer Groups and Congregations

START by forming a safe and trusting clergy peer group that creates a liminal space

Within the group, practicing narrative conversations characterized by not-knowing and curiosity

Finding one's own story in early memories, family genograms, case presentations of leadership, poetic analysis of something you've written or recorded

Building peer companionship that works against clergy isolation and loneliness

Bringing congregational leadership problems to the group through case presentations and open conversations

The group responding playfully to different congregational situations—laughing, lowering anxiety, not taking themselves too seriously

Exercising narrative leadership in congregations guided by the practices of curiosity and not-knowing

Reflecting on these narrative leadership activities in the group; the group asking curious questions, thickening stories of effective leadership

Clergy discovering an increased sense of authenticity; a commitment to facilitating processes more than being wedded to outcomes

Figure 5.1

available." Committees were formed, studies done, and enthusiasm grew among the members of the congregation about the possibilities this new building would bring. It was an exciting time, until seemingly out of the blue the decision was made that the price was too high and that they could wait. And wait they did—more than twelve years!

The gates to the parking lot that the members had been allowed to use freely before were closed, chained, and locked. A large sign advertising that the building was for sale was placed at the corner. Everyone wondered, Why doesn't the church buy it? This included me when I first saw the building and that sign as I drove up to see my new appointment. Everything about purchasing that building made absolute sense. What was going on?

I didn't pursue it much over the first year and half of my appointment, but then I began *to ask curious questions.* "Can you tell me about that building next door?" "Who owns it?" "How long has it been empty?" "Has the church ever thought about purchasing it?" Over and over people told me the story, and it always seemed to end with a sense of frustration with the way the narrative had turned out.

I continued to ask curious questions that were a little more focused, "Where do you see our church being in ministry in the days ahead?" "Would owning that property help us provide effective ministry in this place?" "What do folks think about buying that building today?" "Who do we need to help have that conversation?"

Before I knew it people were beginning to engage me and others in conversation about the purchase of the property. The trustees formed a committee to have the conversation with the property owner. A proposal to purchase the property was presented to the congregation, and overwhelmingly (only three negative votes out of more than two hundred people present and voting) they voted to purchase the property.

It all began with asking curious questions that began to thicken the narrative that no one was pleased with. That produced the alternative narrative of us being committed to being in ministry in this location for the foreseeable future. The building is ours.

Ben adopted three of the most valued narrative strategies among the clergy in this project: *asking curious questions* (rather than giving directions), *thickening a narrative,* and *finding an alternative narrative.* Our emphasis had been on thickening *preferred narratives.* In this case Ben chose to *thicken a failed narrative* and one the congregation didn't want. Using curious questions he got people into conversation about the failed narrative. As they exhumed and rehearsed the story, their dissatisfaction with it deepened and a determination arose to write an alternative narrative. Asking curious questions that thickened a narrative and nurtured an alternative one had become second nature to Ben as he made numerous trips around the circle of reciprocal relationships between his clergy group and his congregation (see Figure 5.1).

It's Made My Work More Authentic and More Difficult

Will describes how his involvement in narrative clergy peer groups has led to increased tension between himself and some members of the congregation. He says, "I believe the project has helped me be more comfortable in taking a 'not-knowing' stance." Although this way of leading feels more congruent to his values, he says, "this has also been difficult for me and for my congregation, who often want me as pastor to be 'the expert and tell them the answer.'" Although it has made his life more difficult, he says it has helped him be more authentic. "There are those in my congregation who are unhappy with what they perceive as my 'lack of leadership' when I don't give them easy answers to their questions or 'tell them what they must do' in my sermon. It upsets some listeners to hear a non-conventional interpretation of a scriptural narrative."

Will bears witness to the fact that narrative leadership goes against the grain of conventional wisdom about leadership, and it often produces resistance. There's a price to be paid for it. Yet, he feels his narrative leadership is a path toward greater authenticity. His ability to risk narrative leadership is supported and reinforced by his peer group. His trips around the circle have reinforced his resolve to stay on a narrative path.

A Lone Ranger Invites Others to Join Him

What difference has this project made in your leadership as a minister? we asked. Gene said it has made his leadership more inclusive and conversational.

> I have always tended to carry out my pastoral responsibilities as a lone ranger, believing I can do them better and faster. So, for twenty-five years I have designed our worship services with input only from the music director. The collaborative process of this project helped me to start a worship planning team three years ago that included members from the congregation. I decided at the outset not to be wedded to the outcome, and I entered into a monthly planning session with the team, which has produced

a much improved worship service that is much more sensitive to the needs of the congregation. Changes have occurred that would not have occurred if I had continued to design worship essentially alone.

Gene adds that this change in his leadership style has led him to "lead the church board in its goal-setting responsibility in a much more collaborative method, what I like to call conversational."

Gene risked changing a twenty-five year practice of planning worship alone to ask laypersons to join him in the task. He was intentional about *not being wedded to the outcome of the planning*. Gene has been involved in three successive narrative clergy groups. In these groups he has experienced a collaborative process—the flexibility of peer group leaders to change the agenda in response to needs of the participants, for example. He saw the leaders let go of the need to reach their desired outcome—at times not without a struggle. And he saw good outcomes, even if not always ones he had anticipated. This group process helped him see an alternative way of preparing for worship, and, for that matter, leading the church board.

Changes in Theological Outlook

We asked participants, Has the project had an effect on your theology? Their accounts varied widely, yet there is one primary thread running through them, which we will consider at the end of this section. First, their stories:

My Formal and Functional Covenants with God

We asked participants to consider their formal and functional covenants with God as a way to help them describe their theology. Their *formal covenant with God* is what they formally profess to others and themselves. Their *functional covenant with God* is the way they actually think and act. Sandra reflected on this exercise about four years after we had used it in her clergy peer group:

I remember talking at one of our meetings about the "heresy of exceptionalism." It is the idea that we have a formal covenant with God that we publicly say we believe. But in actuality we operate out of a functional covenant—that what applies to everyone else just doesn't apply to me. My formal covenant states that "God has not called me to the ministry to be perfect, just faithful." I work under a functional covenant that says, however, "You'd better not mess up. One mistake and you're a failure, and furthermore your calling to the ministry is called into question." I've operated under that functional covenant most of my ministry so that it is hard for me to relax and enjoy my work for fear that I might mess up, or make someone mad to the point that they can justify me packing up and leaving to start all over at another church where I might make a mistake and mess up and be forced to move yet again. Through the combination of this project along with thirty years of ministry behind me I am less anxious about starting my ministry in my new appointment. I am amazed at how relaxed I am already getting with my members. I usually guard every word cautiously, but now I find myself kidding around with members and acting like I've been here for years. Of course, this may all turn around and bite me in the butt, but at this point, what can they do to me? I've decided I don't have anything more to prove and I'll just enjoy serving the church I've been sent to. I've been faithful to God's calling upon my life.

Sandra moves from a theology of works and perfection to a theology of grace and faithfulness. She is living more out of a narrative perspective that does not demand a relentless race toward a goal of success but rather a relaxed and curious and playful journey with her parishioners.

Others Were Pastors to Me

"My theology has expanded. Through the project my peers became priest to me during my battle with cancer. A Catholic mass was held for me. I was on several denominational prayer lists. I was named in a prayer for healing by our rabbi. It was a fresh glimpse of God, and I will be eternally grateful." Sadie added to this the memory that before her surgery everyone in the group had signed a T-shirt with their names and words of prayer and support. She wore the shirt into surgery. "You literally wrapped me," she said. "That's the church of God. And till we've experienced it ourselves, how do we lead it?"

Sadie's words resonate with those we just heard from Sandra, who said her functional theology made her an "exception" to a covenant with a gracious God. She imparted grace to others but couldn't accept it for herself. Sadie, too, made herself an exception. In her case it was an exception to being cared for. She is a skilled pastor with a profound ability to empathize with others and to minister to people with the most perplexing problems. But she seldom experienced that care coming back to her. Something different happened to her in her clergy peer group. She was the recipient of generous and thoughtful care. That reversal had an effect on her theology.

God's Agency and My Agency

"I think the project has had a big effect on my understanding of God's agency and human agency in the world," writes Kay.

> I understand that God is at work in the world. I am a participant in that work, but the work is not "up to me." I can take a curious, open stance toward the way in which the divine is unfolding, but I am not responsible for the outcome. I am responsible for my own actions and my response to God's grace, but ultimately God works through my imperfections. In this way I can see my congregation as a community of faith called forth into the world to show God's grace, rather than as an organization I must "herd" or "direct" along a certain path to success. For example, as I lead the church in evaluating the previous ministry plan and in developing a new ministry plan, I view the leaders as participants in

God's work in the world. God's work is constantly unfolding, and we are privileged to be part of it. Recently I helped the lay leaders review the last ministry plan. I feel that my stance of openness to the way God is leading helps me be a non-anxious presence, rather than a leader who is intent on doing things a certain way.

Kay uses the metaphor of "agency" to clarify her theology—how to exercise her agency to lead and yet yield the outcome to God's agency. It is a matter of joining God's work and being relieved of the burden of trying to create it herself.

Admitting That We Don't Know

Jim says,

> I think the project, along with age and experience, helped me see that leadership may be knowing how to help the congregation find an answer but not necessarily supplying an answer. Process is as vital as outcome. A year or so ago we had to decide if we wanted to jump into the second phase of our building project. No one wanted to say no (which seemed to amount to lack of faith) and no one wanted to say yes (which seemed foolish given the economy and our recent giving). Finally, I challenged the leadership to admit we don't know what to do and tell the congregation. But we would lead the church in a time of discernment, and we did. It was long and at times messy. And in the end we said "No, we need to wait." But it came after everyone felt heard and after a long enough time so everyone felt they hadn't been rushed to a decision.

The major theological shift in Jim's ministry was to change from commitment to a particular *outcome* to guiding a *process* to reach a decision. He had learned narrative ways to facilitate the process— take a not-knowing position, stay curious, draw out stories from the congregation, look for alternative narratives, and trust God to take the congregation where they need to go. His leadership in this case helped the congregation to decide against a building expansion. This decision is a notable exception to congregations that set out to build but can't raise the money and view the situation as a failure. In Jim's case we hear no but not failure.

Seeing God as More Inclusive

In answer to the question about the project's effect on his theology, Will said, "Yes. I am not sure exactly how, but I feel God is more inclusive than I previously believed. Some time ago an angry member walked out on my sermon and slammed the door when I talked about God's inclusive love, 'even' of illegal immigrants. When I used the example of Jesus opening his ministry to the most neglected and powerless, that was the point of the angry walk out. He has not returned since that sermon."

Will brought home the essence of Jesus's inclusion of marginalized people by seeing in that inclusion a call to care for illegal immigrants. The angry exit of the man was a visible and audible exclamation point to Will and the congregation that this inclusive theology goes against the grain of conventional wisdom and can get you into trouble—which is the same sort of trouble Jesus got himself into. This man is "a friend of tax collectors and sinners."[1]

Evelyn, a Jewish rabbi, also said her theology had become more inclusive. "This project was my first opportunity to interact with so many members of the Christian faith." When she completed her participation in the project group, she signed up for several quarters of clinical pastoral education in local hospitals. There she was "called upon to minister to and be part of many interfaith and Christian families. My interaction with the project group gave me insight into the yearnings of people of other faiths, and I came to see certain forms of worship as expressions of that yearning. The result has been that when I have participated with and ministered to Christian people, I am able to draw upon the parallel yearnings in both my faith and theirs for comfort, for rest, for joy, and for tenderness."

Will and Evelyn took part in different narrative clergy groups, but both groups were interfaith—including Jewish, Protestant, and Catholic participants. Month after month, engagement in these diverse groups pushed against the envelope of their usual thought and practice. Familiar theological ideas were tested and revised.

Got Me Out of My Study

"My theology has moved from stressing theological clarity and doctrinal purity to Jesus's command to love one another and to love and pray for enemies"—that's Gene's statement of the project's effect on his theology.

> When religious people stress theological identity and doctrines that express that identity, they usually end up fighting; when they stress what this identity is supposed to produce in the world, namely loving neighbor and trying to build human community, we approach the kind of unity I believe God desires. In a personal way, this has forced me out of my study and into the world. I have organized and personally participated in about a half a dozen mission projects, including traveling to the Gulf Coast to help rebuild houses destroyed by Hurricane Katrina. This immersion in mission has created deepened relationships with members of the church and helped our congregation increase our mission in the world.

We might say that Gene's change in theology expresses his movement from intellectual work to soul work. The soul work is his engagement—for himself and his congregation—in mission to care for suffering people. Theological exactness has given way to loving his neighbor and building human community.

The Theological Thread of Not-Knowing

Not-knowing runs as a thread through these testimonies of theological change. It is in fact at the root of all of these changes. When you take a not-knowing position, you break out of the theology of conventional wisdom, which is *a knowing theology.* It is a theology of certainty. It is prescriptive. It calls for leaders to move people toward goals the leader has devised. We hear from these ministers an alternative theological narrative of curiosity that embraces the uncertainty of trusting God.

Sandra's change in theology, reflected in her comparing her formal and functional covenants with God, lies in her tempering the attempt to be perfect—a knowing position—and embracing instead the task of being faithful. Sadie stepped into a not-knowing position when she allowed others to care for her—care that expanded her experience of church. This required a theological reorientation, because like most clergy, Sadie is practiced at giving care, not receiving it for herself. Kay takes a not-knowing position as she attempts to exercise her own agency and yet trust God's agency for the outcome.

Jim helps church leaders admit to the congregation that *they don't know what to do* about the second phase of the church's building project. He leads them to devise a discernment process, one that ends up being messy, in which the congregation as a whole answers the question. Will and Evelyn take not-knowing adventures to develop a more inclusive theology, one that gets a door slammed in Will's face. Gene turns from a knowing effort to achieve theological exactness to the not-knowing adventure of leading members of his church in cleaning up the messes of human tragedy.

Three Kinds of Ignorance

James Carse, in his book *The Religious Case against Belief,* uses the term "ignorance" to describe what we've called "not-knowing." He says that at the heart of every great religion is a mystery the followers cannot understand. Yet, they can't cease trying to understand it. Nonetheless it is *unknowable.* We must, he says, integrate this unknowability into our conception of religion. "This can have a strong effect on our thinking in general: reflecting on the remarkable way the great religions seem to develop an awareness of the unknown keen enough to hold its most ardent followers in a state of wonder, we may begin to acquire the art of seeing the unknown everywhere, especially at the heart of our most emphatic certainties. This is not just to develop a new intellectual talent, but to enter into a new mode of being, a 'higher ignorance.'"[2] This higher ignorance is, he says, one of three kinds of ignorance[3]:

1. *Ordinary ignorance* is what we experience every day. The church computer network shut down, but we're ignorant of the cause. The church budget has fallen short, but we are ignorant of the reason for it. We are ignorant of how the congregation will respond to the sermon we are about to preach.

2. *Willful ignorance* is when we are aware there's something we don't know and we choose not to know it. A family refuses to acknowledge the damage being done by a member's alcoholism. A suburban congregation with dwindling membership doesn't want to learn about the ethnic minorities who have arrived to occupy their once all-white neighborhood.

3. *Higher ignorance* is an ignorance that can only be learned. It is a process of awakening to the limitations of our knowledge. "Galileo was dedicated to the truth however it emerged. But what we see in his life is that there is no end of truths, and not one of them beyond challenge. There is always something new and unexpected to be learned. What drove him, in other words, was not his knowledge but his ignorance. He *knew* that he did not know. He also knew he never would know all." His higher ignorance "shows itself most obviously in his indefatigable curiosity, an inquisitive search for new truths, a search made possible only by learning the depth of his own ignorance."[4]

Effects of Narrative Leadership on Congregational Cultures

When ministers assume a *higher ignorance,* when they approach their leadership from *a not-knowing position,* they invite cultural change. By culture we mean the rich network of symbols, language, and behavior that define a particular human community.[5] "The theological thread of not-knowing" we have described above is central to congregational cultural change. It goes against *the modern knowing culture* that expects clear answers and definitive solutions. Ministers who exercise narrative leadership are pursuing "a higher ignorance."

Another way to distinguish between a narrative leadership of not-knowing and leadership that embraces the culture of certainty is to distinguish between technical solutions and adaptive responses to problems.[6] Technical solutions derive from a clearly-defined problem and lead to a clearly-defined answer. Adaptive responses are more profound and seldom clear and certain. They can loosen deep cultural roots, such as the fusion of patriotism with Christianity. Barbara's way of dealing with the gift of an American flag to be placed "on the right hand of the altar" was an adaptive response that could lead to a cultural change in the congregation. It could eventually evoke a cultural shift acknowledging that the United States is not a "Christian nation" but rather made up of many different religious faiths whose freedom to worship is guaranteed by the Constitution.

Anthony Robinson in his *Transforming Congregational Culture* says that "in more stable times, or when one is dealing with routine or technical problems, leaders typically provide direction by giving answers and furnishing solutions." These are not stable times, he says. We are in the midst of cultural changes that require a different kind of leadership. These changes are adaptive challenges, and they require leaders who do more than provide solutions to technical problems. *These leaders need "a quite different, and more challenging, skill: asking questions,"* he says. "Sometimes the questions that need to be asked are quite simple. But while the questions may be simple or basic, the answers are not."[7] When ministers in these narrative clergy peer groups took a not-knowing position, operating out of a higher ignorance, they moved beyond technical solutions to address adaptive challenges.

Knowing Your Story and Leading with It

In chapter two, "How Can You Know Your Story?" we referred to Diana Butler Bass and her research into vital mainline Protestant congregations. Recall what she had learned: that effective clergy leaders know their story and lead with it. They exercise "narrative leadership."[8] She said, "Some people know stories and tell them well but live without intentional connection to those stories; others simply experience the quotidian life with no reflection on larger stories of meaning. In vital mainline churches leaders knew their stories and lived them—thus turning the power of narrative into a source of and resource for change."[9] Understanding and leading with one's personal story and taking a not-knowing position go hand-in-hand. When clergy know their stories, they become more secure in their own skin. As they have told us, they have a greater sense of authenticity—they are self-defined. This gives them the freedom to embrace diversity and enables them to appreciate the authenticity of other people and groups. What leads others to take the positions they do? What are the deep resources of their thought and action? Clergy seek answers to these questions by embracing a higher ignorance. In this venture they touch the deep roots of congregational culture. Here are accounts of ministers who, in their authenticity and not-knowing, touched the cultural roots of congregations and educational institutions.

Testimony about a Personal Spiritual Practice

"When I began this clergy group six years ago, the invitation to explore some early memories emboldened me to take a different tack with my ministry. I began telling my story in the pulpit." Gene continues,

> For over twenty years I had been preaching to my congregants the importance of good stewardship practices in one's life of faith and service. I had appealed to all the standard biblical passages and theological reasons for being generous toward God with our time, talent, and finances. In recent years I had been stressing tithing as a goal for all of us. I have been tithing for twenty years, but I have never had the courage to share this information with the congregation, either in private conversations or sermons.
>
> One particular Sunday the Spirit moved me to tell the story of how I started tithing. I was sitting on a bench at a bus stop outside of Boston with my best friend waiting for a bus, and out

of the blue he asked if I tithed. I told him that I was striving to do so but actually gave only about eight percent of my income to the church. He looked at me and said, "What is stopping you from giving another two percent?" I didn't have an answer for that, so that fall I began tithing and have never stopped.

I shared that story with the congregation and challenged ten people to become new tithers that year, and if within the first ninety days they had any regrets for any reason, they could let the treasurer know and we would revise their pledge downward and refund the difference that they had already paid. It was both a tremendous breakthrough for me personally and for the church budget. I discovered the power of personal narrative in preaching, which has revolutionized my style of ministry, especially preaching and worship leadership.

Gene's personal story drew people toward a cultural shift in congregational stewardship that hours of rational biblical persuasion had failed to produce. He learned his story and risked leading with it.

Pastoral Care That Doesn't Fix the Problem

Sally, who moved from a career as a computer programmer into ministry, tells this:

Our basic rules in the clergy group include no fixing, no advising, no solving. In place of solutions, we seek to ask curious questions to help each other discover another way of looking at a problem. These are practices I use frequently when talking with a person one-on-one. Prior to the project I used to dread when someone stopped by the office "just to talk." I usually knew they were wrestling with some difficult problem, which they expected the pastor to fix or solve. I dreaded these encounters because I in no way felt equipped or capable to do so. Now I see these conversations differently. I see my role as one of listening and asking questions to help the person see an alternative story or approach they may have been unable to see without the questions. I try to help them see a different side of the story or a more hopeful narrative by asking questions. The project has helped free me from the burden of having to fix everyone's problem and instead help them discover within their story what they need to move forward.

She tells about a woman who came to talk with her about her older teenage son, who lived away from home and had called her to tell her he had a problem with addiction. This mother prayed frequently about her son's problems and concluded that she was to blame for them—something was wrong with her either as a Christian or as a mother. Sally asked curious questions that led the mother to see an alternative narrative—that the problem belonged to her son and not to her. The questions helped this mother see that his call for help wasn't uncommon for people his age, that he showed wisdom in realizing he was in over his head. Moreover he had enough trust in her to tell her the truth about his situation. With Sally's questions the mother also made note of the fact that she had set firm conditions for his living at home, one more clue to an alternative story about her as a mother.

This pastoral care response wasn't the expert pastor telling the mother what she needed to do. It wasn't the expert counselor delving into her past. It was a compassionate partnership with a pastor who asked thoughtful, curious questions. The woman sought a technical answer to her problem, "What am I to do about my son?" Sally asked curious questions that opened up the possibility that this was an adaptive challenge for the mother to rethink the nature of her relationship with her son. It moved toward a change in the family culture.

Education That Takes Students on Narrative Ventures

Sadie, the Minister to the University, tells this story about teaching a religion class. She assigned the students the homework of drawing their family genogram. She said, "I wanted to help them see that everyone they minister to will come with their own family system. You are working with the person in front of you and all their past and present." On the spur of the moment she asked if anyone wanted to present their genogram to the class before they turned it in. "One student stood and gave a pretty bleak display. The room got very sober, and I said, 'What did you learn about you from this assignment?' And she said, 'That I don't really have a family and that I'm so glad I'm here because I'm starting to see that I have the power to change the cycle.' The next student had put the symbol for lesbianism on the circle that represented herself and said she was dealing with this. And it went on and on." Sadie said that as the class came to a close "I had to do a major 'this is sacred ground' intervention because people have shared their raw stories and we don't go from here to talk about it!" She got a confirmation of confidentiality from each person in the class. "About the class one student said, 'I have never had such an experience of honesty in my whole life.'"

Her class was an adaptive intervention in teaching that led students into their own stories and stories of their classmates. It was a departure from the established cultural story of teaching and learning in which knowledge is handed down from professor to student. One student discovered she had the power to change her destructive family cycle. Another was awed by the level of honesty in the classroom conversation. And the teacher was herself taken by surprise by the class response.

Jim led a group of divinity students that met weekly for a year in a required practicum in spiritual formation. He says,

In my first year I tried to lecture (informally) and employ normal teaching methods (definitions, recognized approaches, etc.). It made for a very vanilla experience.

This year I've given more time to catching up on what's going on in each other's lives. I sort of kick around the corners, asking things like: "That's interesting. Why do you think that happened?" Or, "Why do you think you're anxious about that?" In a casual way I want to communicate that nearly everything that happens is fodder for the formation of the spirit. After twenty to thirty minutes of this a student will then give his or her story. Afterwards we are free to ask about things that grabbed our ear or heart but no judgment statements or fixing problems. It makes for a more effective and enjoyable time. I also think it shows how to attend to our spirits and others' spirits in a helpful, healthy manner.

Jim, like Sadie, broke out of the culture of conventional academic structures. They both invited students to lead with their own stories, and they let go of the need to know what would happen next. Instead of predictable outcomes, they got surprises as they helped students delve into their own narratives.

Kept Me in Ministry

Three participants reported that the project and their adoption of narrative leadership had kept them in ministry.

"The project group has been different from all other clergy groups I've been in," Ben recalled.

We had a Jewish rabbi, Baptist, Presbyterian, United Methodist, non-denominational, African-American, male, female, heterosexual, and homosexual members. We did not form a group right away. It took time for trust to build and all of us to come on board with the narrative idea of process. I was most appreciative of the mentoring aspect of the project and am convinced that this piece and the group's faithfulness helped to keep me in ministry at a particularly trying time. Our basic rule of "no fixing, no saving, no advising, no setting anyone straight" helped me to find an alternative narrative for personal ministry.

When we asked clergy to respond to questions about their experience in the project, we asked as a final question: "If the above questions haven't done it, dream up a question you would like to be asked about your experience in the project and answer it." Larry wrote this question: "Imagine, if you can, your story in ministry today if you had not engaged in the project experience." "The answer is simple," he said. "I doubt I would be in congregational ministry today."

Kay tells of difficulties in her life during the time she was in the group.

> I was going through a divorce and under pressure from the senior pastor to find a new call. The confidence I gained from the group's support enabled me to succeed in my new calling even under the pressure of my ex-husband's marriage and conflict over custody of our children. This group has been a key to my success in finding a new call. It enabled me to land a position as head of staff in a thousand-member church, which is quite rare in my denomination (or any denomination for that matter). I was vulnerable to burn-out and depression. The group enabled me to navigate a difficult time, such that my gifts are not lost to the church. I have been able to pass through treacherous waters with a lifeboat.

Kay also reports that the narrative approach to leadership has helped her "approach ministry with much less anxiety."

At a critical point in their lives, the project provided these ministers with a community of support and a chance to practice narrative conversations. They stayed in ministry and have become agents to open the door for God's agency to change the culture of their congregations.

The Infectious Power of Not-Knowing

In this chapter we have seen how clergy in these peer groups testify to the power of not-knowing. They have embraced a higher ignorance. And instead of just giving answers to technical problems, they are responding to adaptive challenges—challenges that go to the roots of congregational cultures.

They have drawn from the collective power of their groups so that we now can see the reciprocal relationship between participation in a clergy peer group dedicated to narrative practice and narrative congregational leadership. This circle of their interaction with the group and then with their congregations strengthened their muscle memory of how to exercise narrative leadership. The group offered a place for them to tell about their actions as narrative leaders and receive the support of clergy peers who are practicing the same kind of leadership. The peer groups have been vital to their success as narrative leaders.

As they take a not-knowing leadership position, clergy enter a different theological landscape in which they pursue curiosity instead of certainty. They deepen their appreciation for and experience of mystery and wonder. Instead of pressing people toward a goal, they trust God's work in the congregation—God's agency and not their own. Narrative practice, we have seen, invites theological reflection and opens the door to theological changes that go beyond conventional wisdom.

The stories these clergy tell us bear witness that narrative leadership from a not-knowing position can have a transforming effect on the minister, the congregation, and the congregation's culture.

CHAPTER 6 |

Forming and Leading Narrative Clergy Peer Groups

If, by now, you find yourself drawn toward narrative leadership, you may be wondering how to proceed. How do you go from reading about this to doing it? In our account of narrative leadership we have said:

- Know your story and lead with it.
- There's always more than one story.
- Take a not-knowing position.
- No fixing, saving, or advising.
- Seek transformation not success.
- Participate in a group of clergy peers.

The first five of these perspectives are difficult to maintain without the sixth one—participating in a group of clergy peers. This chapter is a guide for developing and sustaining such a group.

In our work we formed groups of six to nine clergy from different denominations and faiths. That seemed to work well in part because the group existed outside the politics of a particular denomination. Saying this doesn't rule out the possibility of a group of clergy from the same denomination working well together. A church staff can form a group. And different elements of narrative leadership can be adopted for use in existing groups. Once you are clear about the essentials of narrative leadership, there are many different paths to secure the peer group support you need. One participant introduced the reflecting team case method to his local ministerial association, which stimulated their interest in narrative and opened the way for them to further explore narrative approaches.[1]

The Landscape of Narrative Group Process

As you consider forming a narrative clergy peer group or introducing narrative practices into an existing group, consider the metaphor of *landscape* as a reference point to guide the formation of the group. A landscape presents different features of narrative practice without putting them into a linear, step-by-step sequence. A group can take the different features of the landscape and weave them into their own collective group narrative.

The landscape of narrative group process as we describe it here includes eight groups of landscape features. The features overlap, and just as in a natural landscape they can't be neatly separated. Together these eight landscape features form the outline of this chapter (see figure 6.1).

Hospitality

Attention to Context

Kelli and Dick were invited by a denominational judicatory to lead a retreat for clergy introducing them to narrative leadership. The date had been set months earlier, and it dawned on us late in our preparation that we would begin this retreat on November 4, 2008, the night of a historic U.S. election. How would we get the retreat going when the whole world was fixated on who would be elected President of the United States? As Kelli put it, "We're trying to launch this thing when there's an elephant and a donkey in the room!"

This is what we did. After a brief introduction, we acknowledged the elephant and the donkey in the room and said, "This election is a contest of contending narratives of reality, contrasting

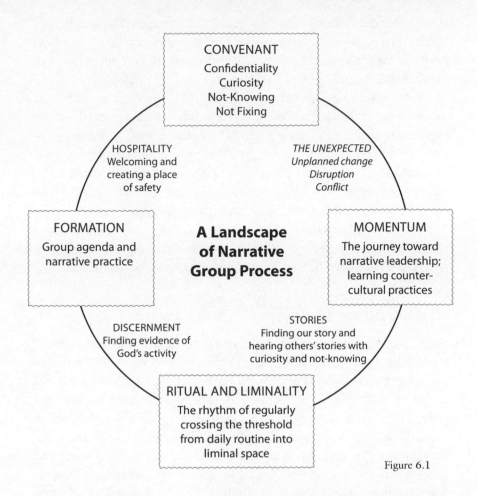

CONVENANT
Confidentiality
Curiosity
Not-Knowing
Not Fixing

HOSPITALITY
Welcoming and
creating a place
of safety

THE UNEXPECTED
Unplanned change
Disruption
Conflict

FORMATION
Group agenda and
narrative practice

**A Landscape
of Narrative
Group Process**

MOMENTUM
The journey toward
narrative leadership;
learning counter-
cultural practices

DISCERNMENT
Finding evidence of
God's activity

STORIES
Finding our story and
hearing others' stories with
curiosity and not-knowing

RITUAL AND LIMINALITY
The rhythm of regularly
crossing the threshold
from daily routine into
liminal space

Figure 6.1

stories of 'This is the way the world is.' Each side in this election has gathered up pieces of information and woven them together into a narrative that serves its purpose. In this process much information has been left behind on the cutting room floor. Each side selects, shapes, and fits together the pieces it chooses." We gave two other examples of this process. We noted that when people write a history of an era, they cannot possibly include all the information available. Even if they could gather it all, they would create a tome no one would want to read. So they must select what's to be included, and they choose the pieces that fit their view of what's important and what's not. We called attention to the four Gospels as examples of this process and the fact that the canon has preserved four different stories of Jesus—each from a different author who had a distinct point of view. None of these accounts, nor all four together, can possibly tell the whole story of Jesus.

Finally, we said that the elephant/donkey narratives were large *macro stories* but that in this retreat we were going to concentrate on the *micro stories* of their personal narratives and how these stories can empower their leadership. We were able to hold their attention for an hour and a half. Then we adjourned to watch the election returns.

The act of contextualizing the retreat in the larger national story was an expression of hospitality. It was a way of inviting people into the room and into their own story without breaking the continuity with the larger narrative that captivated everyone's attention.

A Place at the Table

Food is a central metaphor and substance of hospitality. Communion—the Lord's Supper, the Eucharist—is central to Christian worship. Behind this practice are Jesus's acts of gathering people around a table for a common meal. In chapter four we discussed how, in his meal practice, Jesus was enacting an ancient Hebrew tradition in which every meal was a sacrifice to God. A fundamental characteristic of these ancient meals was hospitality. Jesus extended this hospitality as a host at his table. His open invitation to meals was an affront to the cultural practices that used meals to separate people by rank, status, and purity. Jesus challenged the critics of his open meals by saying, "John the Baptist has come eating no bread and drinking no wine, and you say, 'He has a demon'; the Son of Man has come eating and drinking, and you say, 'Look, a glutton and a drunkard, a friend of tax collectors and sinners!'"[2]

The narrative practice of hospitality is expressed through shared food and drink and equality among the participants. You could have the pastor of a Methodist two-point charge and the Dean of an Episcopal cathedral sitting beside each other, and in this setting they are equals. The power of hospitality puts them at the same level.

The awareness of the depth of the metaphor and substance of food awakens leaders and participants to the importance of other details—welcoming acts of inclusion; a clean, uncluttered, and comfortable setting; touches of beauty; and protection from outside intrusions. At each of our group meetings we had a meal together and enjoyed the rich mix of conversation and good food. It was enacted nourishment, equality, intimacy, and a sense that there was always enough.

Purpose of the Group

Part of hospitality is opening a conversation about the purpose of the group. For example: "The purpose of this group is to give us ministers a place to tell our story, the narrative that is our life, to explore how our story equips us to be narrative leaders, and to create a safe community where we can say whatever is on our minds and hearts. What are your thoughts about this statement of purpose? Does it fit your needs? What changes would you make in it?"

Getting Acquainted

Giving people time and a process for getting acquainted extends hospitality. These are some narrative paths for people to first get to know each other.

- Ask people to get in pairs for three-minute conversations to discuss questions offered by the facilitator. The facilitator keeps time and calls for changing partners every three minutes. Questions can include: "What led you to join this group?" "What story has interested you lately—from a book, movie, TV series, news event, or the like?" "Who are the people in your family?" "What do you most enjoy about your work?"
- Invite participants to tell about *other small groups* they've been a part of. What groups did they like? What made them positive experiences? After a story is told, invite members to ask curious questions of the speaker.

- Invite participants to tell a story about an *ordaining moment*—a time when they felt something like, "Yes! This is why I'm doing the work of ministry."[3] Follow the same pattern of telling the story and inviting questions.

Covenant

The act of hospitality expands as the group establishes a covenant of how they will work together. You can provide a draft and invite recommendations for changes, additions, and deletions. Do not, however, give up what you believe to be the essential elements for a narrative group such as those shown in the *Landscape of Narrative Group Process* (Figure 6.1).

Invite the group to discuss the distinction between *explicit* and *assumptive* covenants. If the covenants are assumed, then there are multiple and invariably conflicting expectations about the purpose of the group and the way people will interact. Explicit covenants help people decide together why they are meeting, how they will interact, and how they will make decisions together.

The covenant is a living document. The printed form of it reports its life at a particular time. It is important, therefore, to visit it periodically to see if it has changed.

If someone breaks the covenant or if the group as a whole strays from it, then the leader has a responsibility to place the matter before the group and ask how the situation should be handled.

The formal agreement to the group covenant is one of the first steps in building trust that allows people to risk telling the stories of their lives. Groups will vary in the length of time it takes for this trust to develop. The ability of group members to stay curious and abide by the rule of no fixing, saving, or advising heightens the sense of security and encourages participants to trust the group with their stories.

Commitment to confidentiality is the bedrock of a narrative group covenant. Often we've been reminded by participants that this covenant makes it possible for them to tell stories they couldn't tell anywhere else.

Here's an example of a possible written group covenant. Of course, you'll have ideas of your own about what to incorporate to best reflect your group.

A GROUP COVENANT

We agree that we will observe the following covenant in this group:

1. To protect the confidentiality of each participant by promising not to share what anyone says beyond the confines of group meetings unless we receive explicit permission from the person to do so.
2. To stay curious and observe the basic rule of *"No fixing, no saving, no advising, no setting anyone straight."*
3. To welcome silence, meditation, and reflection as ways to discern God's work in ourselves and in the group.
4. To speak one at a time and to listen to others without interrupting.
5. To refrain from side conversations.
6. To stay focused on the issue at hand.
7. To help everyone participate.
8. To recognize that anyone can call a time out if the ground rules are not being followed or if the meeting seems to be at an impasse.
9. To observe time limits.
10. To make decisions by consensus. *Consensus is met when a decision is reached that everyone can live with, support, and help implement.*

The Covenant and God

The "we" in the covenant includes God as a party to it. God is, however, an elusive partner. Where and when and how God may act within or upon the covenant is not predictable. God's part in the covenant is shrouded in mystery. God discloses Godself in narrative; therefore, ongoing, reflective attention to stories—both individual and collective—is more likely than not to create a space for God's disclosure. Stories we call "experience-near" carry the greatest disclosure potential. They are personal, intimate, and specific in detail. They open a space in the group where God may speak.

Recall from the last chapter how Sadie introduced genograms to a university religion class. Students were turning in their assignment to draw a genogram of their own families, and she asked if anyone wanted to present theirs to the class. Those who presented their genograms told intimate stories of their lives, and a shift occurred as an academic class found itself on sacred ground. Sadie named the fact that this was a sacred place and that people's stories had to be protected by confidentiality. The students' personal risk taking opened the way for the class unexpectedly to break through the wall of the ordinary and familiar to God's awaiting presence.

Ritual and Liminality

The group begins and is continually nurtured by hospitality. That hospitality is deepened by the formation of a group covenant. The group covenant prepares the way for a series of regular group meetings. Each of these meetings provides a ritual in which participants cross a threshold from their regular routines and roles into liminal space. Here we return to Victor Turner's understanding of ritual, which we discussed in chapters one and four. Ritual is *"planned or improvised performance that effects a transition from everyday life to an alternative framework within which the everyday is transformed."*[4] A narrative clergy group that helps participants tell their story and learn how that story can empower their leadership is *an improvised performance* that takes ministers out of their established routine and role into an *alternative framework*—what Turner calls a liminal space—within which their everyday way of being and leading may be *transformed*.

Timothy Carson, who has investigated the relationship between Victor Turner's understanding of ritual and pastoral ministry, says that ministers are *liminal beings* (or at least potentially so, we would say). They deal with life transitions as do no other professionals— attending births, marriages, baptisms, confirmations, bar and bat mitzvahs, illness, and death, to name a few. When the physician walks out of the room saying, "There's nothing more I can do," the minister follows to create a liminal space for the dying and the family. "The vocation of religious leader . . . set apart by and for and from the community of faith, is itself a state of permanent liminality," says Carson. "Even as a part of an established community, life is itinerant. . . . [T]he religious leader is a part of yet distinct from the community served."[5]

A narrative clergy peer group offers ritual that provides liminal space for clergy whose vocation is to create liminal space for others. This ritual enables group members to receive for themselves, for their own depleted spiritual reservoir, the liminal experience they regularly give to others.

Our participants have described the liminal quality of group meetings as a "sabbath," a "vacation at the beach," "holy ground," "an escape from congregational demands," "unconditional welcome," "nourishment," and "a place of laughter and shared sorrow."

Stories That Emerge in Liminal Space

The hidden stories in one's life offer a resource for change. In the everydayness of life's routine, these stories usually lie neglected—left behind on the cutting room floor. In these neglected stories one may find unexpected evidence of God's activity.

When Ben recalled his earliest childhood memories, he recovered a story of how he and a companion threw rocks at a hornets' nest—a forbidden activity—and how exciting it was to throw the rocks and run. The rocks, it seems, were not simply stones aimed at the hornets but also missiles aimed at the authority that forbade such exciting exploits. Ben is a leader in his denomination and works hard to be a cooperative team player. His early childhood memory, however, brought out in the liminal space of his clergy group, uncovered another theme in his life. That theme is an unease with establishment power and a desire to not become a captive to it. This memory was a doorway through which he could explore the complicated relationships among himself, God, and his denomination.

How does one enter into a liminal space where participants have the freedom and the awakened curiosity to go looking for forgotten or neglected narratives—stories in which God may be calling them to something new?

Liminal space is space across a threshold. The practice of *lectio divina* at the beginning of group meetings—reading a text three times, with silence between readings, followed by a brief conversation about the readings—is a means of crossing a threshold from the daily routine and into liminal space. This activity allows participants to slow down, sit in silence, and listen to scripture or a poem that draws their attention away from their daily work and toward their inner lives. As they settle into this liminal space, they become more receptive to their stories and the stories of fellow group members.

CALLING OUT THE STORIES

In chapter two, "How Can You Know Your Story?" we have described core activities for drawing out a person's self story. These are ways to uncover forgotten stories through which God may be speaking a refreshing, renewing word.

- Recall your earliest childhood memory.
- Choose one of your favorite biblical narratives and explore the connections you can make between this narrative and your earliest childhood memory.
- Draw and present a genogram of your family over three generations.
- Tell of an experience of being a leader before you were twenty.
- Present cases of your work as a minister using a reflecting team case structure.
- Take a section of something you've written or recorded and subtract words and phrases until you have created a poem.[6]

During the life of the group, participants gather different stories about themselves following a sequence such as that above. They may wonder, however, how the narratives are connected. Our experience is that there's always a connection among a person's various narratives and that the reflection required to find the connection can lead to important discoveries. The unifying force that links them together comes from the fact that all the stories are from the same person's memory. They are psychologically and even physically connected, and together they provide a set of clues to answer the question, "What is my self story?" or "What is the story of my life?"

In 1997 a group of narrative practitioners collaborated to produce a book, *Narrative Therapy in Practice: The Archaeology of Hope*. This metaphor illuminates the process of putting together different stories of one's life. Gerald Monk, one of the authors, develops the metaphor: "With meticulous care and precision, the archaeologist brushes ever so gently over the landscape with an instrument as small as a pastry brush. With these careful movements, she exposes a remnant, and with further exploration, others soon appear. Disconnected fragments are identified and pieced together as the search continues. With a careful eye for the partially visible, the archaeologist begins to reassemble the pieces. An account of events in the life of the remains is constructed, and meaning emerges from what was otherwise a mere undulation in the landscape."[7] An important part of this archaeological process is having a place to tell the narratives from different parts of one's past. Listeners become part of the archaeological team as they listen thoughtfully, respectfully, and with deep curiosity.

RESPONDING TO THE STORIES

Once participants have told their stories, their peers can use narrative strategies to respond in certain ways to enrich the process of piecing together the different parts. Here are listener guidelines.

- Become a fellow archaeologist who looks for clues of hidden or partially visible stories of strength, resilience, and courage. The smallest narrative has value.
- Respect the speaker's story, and handle it with reverence—setting aside the urge to rearrange the story to fit your perspective.
- Stay curious, ask questions, and hold back from making statements in the form of questions.
- Resist the temptation to suggest what a story means.
- Stay curious about small, thin stories that a distracted archaeologist might miss. Ask permission of the speaker to stay with such a story for a few more minutes of wondering.
- Ask about the collection of stories that may have been unearthed. Do they point to an alternative narrative about the person or the situation?

Looking for Stories of Strength

It may seem naive to keep the focus in the group on stories of strength. What about the darker stories of failure, missed opportunity, dead end efforts, betrayal, and weakness in the face of opposition? They are certainly present and exude immense power. In the search for stories of strength, are these other ominous stories to be ignored? The answer is certainly no, they cannot be ignored. The challenge is *how to respond* to the problem stories that participants bring to the table.

When a problem story is told, the medical model of diagnosis and treatment typically exerts its influence. The pull of the scientific method is to examine cases with the questions: Why did this happen? What caused it? It is a deficit-based approach. What did you do that you shouldn't have? What did you fail to do that you should have done? Why did you misread the situation? These questions tend to place blame and lead to a search for the causes of failure so they supposedly can be fixed.

A narrative approach sets aside this familiar pattern of investigation. It investigates the history of the problem narrative but with a different question. *It does not deny the problem story; rather, it wants to know about exceptions to it.* This search is undergirded by the belief that God is constantly at work in every person's life to reveal alternatives to problem-saturated stories, although this divine work may be hidden by other forces.

Recall Sally's story of the mother whose teenage son (who was living away) got into trouble and had come home. The mother's problem-saturated story was her guilt that she'd failed as a mother and as a Christian. All she could see was her failure. Sally asked curious questions about the situation, and little by little an alternative narrative came into view. Her son had trusted her enough to own his problem of addiction. There was a bond of trust between them. Moreover, the mother told of setting limits for his return to her household. This story spoke of the son's honesty and the mother's love and firmness. It began to displace the story of the mother's guilt.

The Reassurance Trap

In the effort to find alternative stories of strength, courage, and resilience, it is easy to slip into the habit of reassurance—telling a person about her perceived strengths in the face of problems. This violates the rule of "no fixing, saving, advising, or setting anyone straight." It fails the test of curiosity. It is important to stay in a not-knowing position and to ask questions rather than doling out reassurance. Reassurance stops the story in its tracks, when what we want to do is invite the storyteller to explore another layer of her story. Instead of saying, "Don't forget how you showed patience and understanding to that cantankerous church member," a more helpful response would be, "How would you describe the way you responded to that cantankerous church member?"

What makes the temptation to reassure so powerful? We instinctively want to eliminate discomfort and pain so we become "helpful." Part of this response may be driven by compassion and perhaps not knowing an alternative response. Another part is our desire to diminish our own suffering. The problem story makes us both uncomfortable, and in that circumstance our mind quickly fills with ideas about how the other person (and ourselves) can get out of this fix. Reassurance is an easy way to dull the pain. "It wasn't all a failure; look what you did . . ." "Yes, but I know what a resourceful person you are and . . ." "Remember how you took care of that other problem . . ." Trying to cure the problem through reassurance seldom helps and often puts distance between you and the other person, who thinks to herself, "He's trying to make me feel better, but he really doesn't understand."

Questions to Avoid and Questions to Pursue

Several times we have reiterated the basic rule of "no fixing, no saving, no advising, no setting each other straight." Here, following our consideration of reassurance, we want to thicken that rule with specific examples of the kinds of questions that can deepen the spirit of not-knowing in the group (see box, page 126).

Formation

In the *landscape of narrative group process* we have considered the welcoming power of *hospitality,* the central place of the *group covenant*, the way each group meeting is contained in *a ritual that opens up liminal space,* and how the essence of group work is *telling and exploring personal stories.* We turn now to *formation.*

By *formation* we mean two things: first, how the group is formed to accomplish its purpose, and second, the way group activity contributes to the personal and professional formation of the participants. These two are interrelated and reciprocal. The way the group is formed makes a difference in the kind of formation work

QUESTIONS TO AVOID	QUESTIONS TO PURSUE
Questions that make judgments. "Why didn't you simply tell him, 'No, I'm not willing to do that?'"	*Questions that aim at understanding the person and not just the situation.* "What makes this story stand out for you at this time?"
Questions that give advice. "What about talking with your district superintendent about this?"	*Questions that seek to discern what the person is asking for*—for example, a solution, empathy, partnership, or consolation. "What would you say you're looking for from us as you tell us this story?"
Questions that offer analysis. "You did what you thought was the best course of action at the time. What more could you have done?"	
Questions that seek to fix. "What about asking yourself, 'Is this really my problem or does it belong to the board?'"	*Questions that invite the person to consider the resources in her own story.* "What's helped you find clarity about such things in the past?"
Questions that attempt to save. "If you keep going down this road, aren't you finally going to come to a dead end?"	*Questions that invite the person to talk about what his story means to him.* "Does this story touch a theme or thread in your life?"
	Questions that wonder about clues to deeper layers of the narrative. "I noticed that your voice got very soft as you told this story. What do you think that's about?"
	Questions that externalize the problem. "You said you feel this heavy weight on you all the time. Is the weight always there, or do you have times when it's not oppressing you?"

the members do. And the experience of group members attending to their own formation shapes the life of the group. In our work as group leaders we have taken the initiative to provide group structure; however, what has happened in the lives of the participants has led us to form and reform the way we lead the group. The changes have not been quick or abrupt but rather gradual and evolutionary. This book is the outcome of this mutual process of formation.

The Group Agenda

The group agenda is part of the formation process, and participants have told us that the meeting agenda is essential to a good group experience. We plan and post an agenda for each meeting. Agendas include:

- Time for participants to tell individual stories
- Collective group-building activities
- Narrative-based learning
- Practice of narrative competencies

The agenda is a *container* for the meeting that creates a sense of security and direction for the day. It is a flexible container. The leader of the group monitors the time against what is happening within the group—and what's happening outside the group that may be affecting it.

Narrative Practices

A clergy peer group is a laboratory for experimentation with narrative practice. In this laboratory these formational practices can occur:

- Using strategies to uncover your own self story—early childhood memories, accounts of leadership before twenty, genograms, and so forth.
- Members following the basic rule as they respond to these stories.
- Case presentations and not-knowing, curious responses from the reflecting team.
- Open conversations that observe the basic rule.
- Looking for alternative narratives to problem stories.
- Thickening thin narratives rather than quickly moving on to someone else's story.

Such narrative practices are difficult because they run counter to conventional wisdom. Conventional wisdom prizes knowing and

AN EXAMPLE OF A TYPICAL GROUP MEETING AGENDA

Desired outcomes for the day [*what you hope group members will carry away from the meeting, in this case a skill and a learning*]:
- Deepened skill at asking curious questions.
- Strategies for leading from a not-knowing position.

Time	Activity	Facilitator
10:00–10:10AM	Gathering: A time of hospitality with snacks and drinks.	In this column list the names of members who are leading that segment of the meeting.
10:10–10:30AM	*Lectio Divina*: A biblical text, a poem, or other piece read three times—each by a different member—with silence between readings. The *lectio divina* provides a transition from the daily work of the participants to the different space of the group—the liminal space.	
10:30–11:15AM	Check in: Allocating a relatively brief time for members to update the group on what's happening in their life (e.g., 5 minutes each). In order for each person to have a fair share of air time, the leader or someone designated needs to keep time. Check in can be opened by a question. Some possible questions: • What do you need to tell us in order to be present today? • What's clearer to you since we last met? • What haunts you? (Good for October)	
11:15AM–12:15PM	Case presentation: Using the reflection team model.	
12:15–1:00PM	Lunch	
1:00–1:45PM	A teaching segment: This can be something presented by the leader or by group members who take turns from meeting to meeting presenting topics such as: • Ways to lead from a not-knowing position • What is a curious question? • The power of an overhearing position	
1:45–2:00PM	Break	

2:00–2:45PM	Open time: Group members can claim time to discuss their concerns. Here, as well as in the case presentation, the temptation will be strong to break the basic rule. People will want to fix, save, advise, and set people straight. Keep the basic rule posted prominently, and call attention to it when people stray from it.
2:45–3:00PM	Reflect on the day: At this point the group stops its forward movement to look back over what has happened during the meeting. It moves to *process* questions such as: • What went well, and what do we need to change to make future meetings better? • Have we achieved the desired outcomes? • How have we done today in holding to the basic rule?

certainty and has little tolerance for ambiguity. Narrative practice values curiosity and not-knowing and is aware that there's always more than one story. It embraces uncertainty and ambiguity. It works in the gap between what happened and what we can recover and tell about what happened. Narrative practice avoids setting up camp on one narrative and is always alert to alternative stories. Taking a not-knowing position is one of the most difficult practices to learn and yet is one of the most useful positions a minister can take as a leader.

The Unexpected

The unexpected appears as an inevitable feature of the *landscape of narrative group process*. The proverb for this is, "Expect the unexpected, and you won't be disappointed." A member comes late because she discovered that the church heating system had quit. (It's 28 degrees outside.) Another calls right at starting time to say his car has broken down. Halfway through the day a group member gets a call from his child who is sick at school and has to be picked up. Another member has to leave early to perform a funeral. Half the group is either absent or there only part of the time. Under such circumstances another proverb fits: "Whoever is here is enough."

Contingencies such as these may call for adjusting the agenda, but by having a planned agenda in advance there is at least a structure that can be adapted. It's not something to be thrown out the window because things seem to be coming unglued. Remarkable things can—and often do—occur under such unexpected circumstances. Dick recalls being on a retreat that was planned for nine colleagues, but only four finally got there. The four survivors were disappointed. The question arose, "What shall we do with just the four of us?" Finally, one said, "What about telling stories about 'ordaining moments' in our lives when we felt deeply, 'Yes, this is what I'm supposed to be doing!'" They spent the retreat telling and exploring these stories and later brought that question back to the rest of the group.

Momentum

The process of formation contributes to momentum. Group members aren't there simply for support—although support is a component. There's movement. The forward movement is provided by the steep learning curve participants face as they develop a narrative approach to leadership. In order to practice narrative leadership, one must loosen the shackles of conventional wisdom. This is difficult. But it can also be exhilarating. Remember Will's statement about teaching a narrative approach to ministers in Central America: "This approach is real countercultural," he said. "It was fun. I began to understand narrative better." Then he said it's "scary" because it is subversive to the powers of the dominant conventional culture.

This way of viewing things calls for clergy to step away from the expert model of leadership to take a different position. John Wimmer, our mentor at Lilly Endowment, tells us this about our approach: "The narrative model has the potential to radically change the way pastors lead. They can give up the façade of knowing it all and become listeners who empower the laity and awaken their gifts for ministry. Pastors do not have all the answers, and acting as if they do could be one of the biggest enemies of pastoral excellence."[8]

Learning to stay curious and practice the basic rule of no fixing, saving, or advising is an immense challenge requiring repeated practice. It is like asking a right-handed person suddenly to start writing with her left hand. Such a challenge provided momentum in our groups because neither participants nor leaders could perfect this art. Learning how to do it never stopped.

Combine this new way of seeing things with an exploration of each person's personal narrative, and the result is a rich and highly challenging learning situation that produces momentum.

The momentum in the groups further expressed itself in the congregations and institutions where these clergy served as leaders. We asked them to tell how they used a narrative approach in their congregations. Being curious and taking a not-knowing position stood out as frequent themes in these stories. This position lowered anxiety and kept clergy in conversation with people when the going got rough. It generated momentum in their congregations as lay persons stepped forward to lead in response to the minister's curiosity. It promoted more egalitarian relationships and shifted the center of gravity away from reliance on the minister as the expert problem solver.

Recall Jim's account of the church's dilemma about moving into a second phase of its building project. "No one wanted to say no (which seemed to amount to lack of faith) and no one wanted to say yes (which seemed foolish given the economy and our recent giving). Finally, I challenged the leadership to admit we don't know what to do and tell the congregation." Jim refrained from taking responsibility to try to figure out which direction to take. Instead, he led by facilitating the process. After a difficult discernment process, the congregation decided to wait on launching the second building phase. In these unfolding events, the momentum became less toward building and more toward greater congregational engagement and the evolution of a decision-making process—one that could also be used in the future when the congregation faced other challenges.

A primary generator of momentum in a narrative clergy group is *the teaching aspect* of each meeting. During this segment of forty-five minutes to an hour, new ideas are introduced and previously introduced ideas are recycled. Repetition of ideas feeds the momentum because the capacity to be a narrative leader comes only with much practice.

Another generator of momentum is *the experience-near stories* the participants tell about themselves. *Experience-near* narratives are personal and specific. Narratives that are not experience-near tell of happenings at a distance from the storyteller and that remove her or him from direct engagement with the events being told. Experience-near stories may express uncertainty, dilemmas, and ambiguity. They may tell of successes or celebrations but also give some sense of the twists and turns it took to get there.

Retelling stories contributes to the momentum, for every retelling is a new edition of a story and a fresh source of revelation about the teller and the group.

The momentum of the group is inward as well as outward. As participants practice narrative strategies in the group, the emotional ties among members are deepened. They tell their stories and are heard with respect and curiosity. They are not told what they should do, which increases intimacy and safety, allowing people to take risks to let others know what's happening in their lives.

Discernment

Discernment is part of the landscape of every group meeting. It begins with not-knowing. It is nurtured by the basic rule: don't fix, don't save, don't advise. Ministers come from their intense, schedule-filled, meeting-driven, last-minute-planning, problem-solving, putting-out-fires daily work. And this call to not-knowing raises the question: "What are we here for if we aren't fixing, saving, or giving advice?" They are here to tell and listen to personal stories. How odd.

In the liminal space of the group, the familiar things that most of the time shape their lives—all those relentless demands—are laid aside. Group members slow down and stop. They are asked to look back into their past and find their earliest childhood memory. In that memory and others like it, discernment occurs. They are surprised to find clues to their present life. And surprised to discover God making Godself known in these ventures into the deep woods of their memory. They tell their stories, and fellow group members wonder with them about what they mean. They notice important details the storyteller has overlooked. "What about this?" someone asks. And the response is, "I hadn't paid any attention to it until you mentioned it."

Our journey into early memories inevitably places us near to God's disclosure, because God has constantly been at work in our life to realize God's dream for us and for humankind. The evidence of God's work has been deposited there. And when we find it, it's not an ancient artifact but rather a present encounter. The encounter may be dramatic or it may be subtle. Or we may miss it altogether. Belonging to a group of fellow clergy who are on the same venture, however, increases the chances of encounter.

Paying Attention to the Gap

We have said that the gap between what actually took place and what people can tell of it is the space where a narrative approach does its primary work. In this gap a curious person can go to that heap of neglected information on the cutting room floor and find other narratives—stories that may reinforce or challenge the one that's been told. *The deepest part of this gap is the difference between what happened and what we are able to gather up and tell ourselves and others about it. No matter how diligent, we cannot collect exactly what happened. This deep gap is the space where God may disclose Godself.* Certainty and the idea that we can state unambiguously what God is up to is dissolved in this gap, and we are left to stand humbly before this mystery as not-knowers. God breathes in this gap,[9] and if we allow ourselves the full experience of waiting before it, we may experience God's presence.

Once Again the Landscape

This chapter is a guide for developing a narrative clergy group. In it we have described a landscape of such a group that includes these eight features:

- Hospitality
- Covenant
- Ritual and Liminality
- Stories That Emerge in Liminal Space
- Formation
- The Unexpected
- Momentum
- Discernment

We hope you will find our description useful for groups you initiate or those you belong to. As you adapt our ideas to fit your particular situation, we expect you will come up with your own narrative ideas and resources. When you do, we would like to hear about them.

The final section of this book, following our conclusion, is a set of resources (handouts) that have helped clergy groups understand various aspects of narrative thought and practice. We hope you will use them and adapt them to your particular needs.

To contact the authors, e-mail us at kelliwj@gmail.com and r.loren.hester@gmail.com.

Conclusion

Know your story and lead with it has been our invitation for you to find the somewhat elusive narrative that describes who you are, your way of doing ministry, and the unfolding direction of your life. Knowing your story, we've said, is an essential component of effective leadership. Finding your story among the myriad narratives that fill your life isn't a simple task. So we have offered a path to find it. We have invited you into a liminal space where we imagine you sitting with a group of clergy colleagues who've made a covenant to meet regularly to explore your personal narratives, to find mutual encouragement, and to learn a narrative way of leading.

Perhaps you don't yet have such a group. Maybe you don't know whether or when that will be possible. In this case we hope that through the medium of this book we can still support and encourage you on a narrative venture. Although you don't have a clergy peer group as we have described it, we believe opportunities for narrative experiences of companionship are close at hand. When you lead from a not-knowing position and listen to people with deep curiosity, doors to companionship can open in unexpected places.

As we looked for role models that demonstrated a narrative way of leading, we "met Jesus again for the first time"[1] to see that he was one who practiced narrative leadership. He delivered his message through stories, and he challenged the prevailing narratives of power and privilege as the Hebrew prophets did before him. He affirmed the little narratives of hope among the peasants against the grand narratives of domination of the ruling classes. In short, he led through narrative.

This book grows out of the stories of ministers with whom we have worked over a period of six years. As they've found ways to lead out of their own stories, they have, in various ways, tapped into the wisdom of Jesus's leadership. We have seen them:

- Define themselves and stay connected to those who oppose them.
- Negotiate difficult situations with confidence as they drew on their story and the story of their congregations.
- Risk leading with curiosity and a not-knowing position even when anxious voices pressured them to be knowers.
- Make clear covenants about how to work together and to hold confidences.
- Embrace sabbath time for themselves and their congregations.
- Draw on the wisdom of their clergy group by calling on each other individually for consultation and by continuing to participate in a narrative clergy group long after their initial two-year experience.
- Become advocates for justice as a mission of the congregation and as a quality of congregational life.
- Dispel anxiety with playfulness and laughter.

Leading through narrative begins with deep curiosity and a willingness to take a not-knowing position. It remembers there's always more than one story. And it knows how to go to the cutting room floor to find forgotten alternative narratives to problem-saturated accounts. It pays attention to the smallest and most humble stories as possible clues to God's ceaseless work and opens the way to participate in God's dream for humankind.

We said at the beginning, "We hope that as you read the book you will have a sense that this is your pilgrimage, too, and we hope that our account will encourage you into narrative ventures of your own." After all, the most important story of this book is not the stories we have told. The most important one is your story and how you are leading with it.

Resources for
Narrative Clergy Groups

The resources that follow are eight outlines drawn from our collection of handouts for narrative clergy groups. They provide compact versions of material in the book in user-friendly formats.

1. Practicing *Lectio Divina*
2. A Group Covenant
3. Finding Your Story
4. Practicing Curious Questions
5. A Reflecting Team Model for Case Presentations
6. Guidelines for Constructing Genograms
7. Collecting and Prioritizing Ideas from the Group
8. Closing a Meeting with Time to Reflect

LECTIO DIVINA

The practice of *lectio divina*, "divine reading," was developed in the monastic tradition. Monastic rules of several orders include it, but the "Rule of St. Benedict" seems to be the one most referenced today. *Lectio divina* is a way of reading scripture. In our use of the practice we read a text three times and allowed for a brief period of silence between each reading.

Traditional practice uses Hebrew and Christian scriptures. We have found that using poetry[1] for the *lectio* reading is also an effective spiritual practice. *Lectio divina* is a way to help people cross a threshold from their everyday life and work to enter a liminal space. There the usual routine is set aside, thoughts and feelings emerge that otherwise are pushed aside in day-to-day work, and space is made for God's spirit.

First Reading

- Let the text wash over you. Don't try to do anything with it. Practice receptivity.
- Silence.

Second Reading

- Listen for a word or phrase that stands out for you. Silently repeat and savor it.
- Silence.

Third Reading

- Consider the question: "Where does this text touch my life, and what might it be calling me to do?"
- Silence.

We conclude with our responses to the *lectio*.

A GROUP COVENANT

We agree that we will observe the following covenant in this group:

1. To protect the confidentiality of each participant by promising not to share what anyone says beyond the confines of group meetings unless we receive explicit permission from a person to do so.
2. To stay curious and observe the basic rule of *"No fixing, no saving, no advising, no setting anyone straight."*
3. To welcome silence, meditation, and reflection as ways to discern God's work in ourselves and in the group.
4. To speak one at a time and to listen to others without interrupting.
5. To refrain from side conversations.
6. To stay focused on the issue at hand.
7. To help everyone participate.
8. To recognize that anyone can call a time out if the ground rules are not being followed or if the meeting seems to be at an impasse.
9. To observe time limits.
10. To make decisions by consensus. *Consensus is reached when a decision is made that everyone can live with, support, and help implement.*

FINDING YOUR STORY

Based on her research into vital mainline Protestant congregations, Diana Butler Bass says that effective pastoral leaders know their story and lead with it. They exercise "narrative leadership."[2] "Some people know stories and tell them well, but," she says, they "live without intentional connection to those stories; others simply experience the quotidian life with no reflection on larger stories of meaning. In vital mainline churches," she concludes, "leaders knew their stories and lived them—thus turning the power of narrative into a source of and resource for change."[3]

Chapter two is a full description of how clergy have become better acquainted with their own story. This is an outline of that process.

It is not easy to know one's story. Our identity is a fabric woven by the strands of many relationships—our parents or parent surrogates being the earliest ones. These strands are the basic stuff we use to fashion our sense of ourselves—who we are and what our purpose in life is. Countless other influences are woven into who we are. But we are very close to the fabric, and it is hard for us to see the whole of it. Here are strategies for seeing the fabric of your story more clearly.

1. What is your earliest childhood memory?

    a. Find a memory you have of a specific event and not "something our family always did."

    b. Choose something *you* recall, not an account told to you by someone else. (You may want to check out the memory with family members, *but don't let go of your original memory.*)

    c. Select a memory that has a narrative plot—a beginning, middle, and end. You know you have a plot when, if you stopped in the middle, a listener would ask, "What happened next?"

    d. Tell your age at the time of the story, describe the setting, record the feelings the story generates, tell what stands out, and tell who the principal characters are.

e. Early memories tend to be more about you in the present than you in the past. You remember them because they resonate with your present outlook and stance toward life. The memory you find may be a less-than-accurate report of what happened. The task is not so much to reach for what actually took place but rather to ask about the metaphorical quality of the memory. What does it portray about you? What does the story say about you as you are today?

f. Early memories have the power to bring to the surface both hopeful and disturbing aspects of one's life. If the story connects with significant past trauma, it is very important to talk about that. If you can't talk about it in a group, then seek out someone you can trust to tell it to.

g. Since our parents or parent surrogates are our earliest images of God, how do you see these God-figures shaping your theology? What have you embraced? What have you worked against?

2. *Choose a favorite Hebrew or Christian narrative, and ask how this story may connect with your early memory. It's not necessary to find a biblical narrative you think fits the early memory.* Simply choose a favorite one and then consider: "How do these two narratives converse with one another?" (Parables are particularly useful narratives for this exploration because they are stories crafted to test other narratives, to open them up for examination. Explore the meaning of the parable through interpreters who take a narrative approach, such as Marcus Borg, John Dominic Crossan, William Herzog, Bernard Brandon Scott, etc.)

3. *Draw a genogram of your family of origin.* A genogram is a family tree that depicts three or four generations—yours, your parents', your grandparents', and possibly the generation before that. The genogram provides a scaffolding to hold the narratives you are working with. It reveals the context in which the early memories took place. Genograms

give you access to family stories out of which you have composed your own self narrative. Presenting the genogram to the group gives you a chance to assemble your family and self stories into a whole story. What theological dimensions do you see in the genogram—both theology you embrace and theology you reject? What theological themes are woven through the generations? (See also "Guidelines for Constructing Genograms" later in this Resources section.)

4. *Recall an incident of your leadership before you were age 20.* This narrative draws upon later memories and narrows the focus to leadership. This narrative gives you a chance to consider:

   a. Agency—your own action—the power to accomplish what you need to do.
   b. How, in this agency, you work with other people.
   c. Whether your story is mainly reacting to circumstances or being proactive to venture into something of your own choosing.
   d. How you understand the relative power of your personal agency and God's agency.

5. *Connect your case presentations to the narratives you have developed so far.* Your case presentations disclose how your story interacts with the stories of your congregation, your community, and your fellow clergy. What connections do you make between your case and the other steps you have taken to discern your self story?

PRACTICING CURIOUS QUESTIONS

Conventional culture resists curiosity, and asking genuinely curious questions isn't an easily acquired skill. Conventional wisdom yearns for answers and certainty. Curious questions open us up to ambiguity and uncertainty. They do not feed the hunger to have everything neatly figured out. Curiosity didn't kill the cat—conventional wisdom did.

1. *Using the subjunctive mood.* Curious questions are usually set in the subjunctive mood rather than the imperative or indicative moods. The indicative and imperative tend to close options and limit responses. The subjunctive mood tends to open possibilities and increase options.

   Indicative: "God is calling us to this new mission."
   Imperative: "We must not shrink back from the opportunity God has given us!"
   Subjunctive: "What if God is calling us to something new?"

   Indicative: "We are concerned that you take care of yourself."
   Imperative: "You must take care of yourself."
   Subjunctive: "What if you asked, 'What is best for me in this situation?'"

   Indicative: "I want us to get some estimates on a new building."
   Imperative: "We are running out of space. We have to build a new building."
   Subjunctive: "When we say we need a new building, I wonder what each of us is thinking. What do we each have in mind?"

2. *Closed vs. open-ended questions:*

   Closed: "Why are the offerings falling short?"
   Open: "I wonder what factors may be contributing to our offerings being lower?"

Closed: "Are you going to use that same hymn for the third time?"
Open: "What about that hymn keeps drawing you to it?"

Closed: "Are you aware that Betty was hurt by what you said to her?"
Open: "I wonder how Betty responded to what you said to her."

3. *To ask curious questions requires a practice that:*

  a. Assumes a not-knowing position and sets aside the need to have answers or be an expert: "Yes, I have my own view of this, and I can share it, but at the moment I'm interested in your view and how you have been dealing with the issue."

  b. Follows the basic countercultural rule of "no fixing, no saving, no advising, no setting anyone straight": "I don't have a solution to this problem. I wonder if you are asking for a partner to help you figure it out."

  c. Sets aside the need to move a person intellectually or emotionally from one place to another—in this case, for example, trying to remove a person's embarrassment: "You were embarrassed and felt bad about that situation. At first glance I can't see a connection between the embarrassment you felt and what you did. How did embarrassment get into this picture?"

  d. Separates the person from the problem: "You're concerned about losing your temper in this situation. Is it unusual for anger to get the best of you, or has anger been after you for a long time?"

  e. Listens for alternative narratives: "You said you felt completely ineffective in the conversation with your boss. You also said he later asked you to give him a copy of the information you'd gathered. I wonder why he asked to see your research."

  f. Aims at thickening the other person's narrative to include more than what may appear in a surface statement:

"You said, 'One day I just walked away from the job.' How were you able to come to the place to say, 'I'm quitting this job!' and walk off from a secure source of income?"

g. Develops an ear for the very small story and is persistent in asking for that story: "You just said you don't feel competent leading worship. Is there a certain part that comes to mind?" "When in the service do you become uncomfortable?"

It's impossible to ask an honest, open question if you think you already know the answer.

A REFLECTING TEAM METHOD
OF CASE PRESENTATIONS

In a reflecting team approach to presenting cases, a person volunteers to tell about a situation for which she seeks consultation. It may be an issue or problem in the congregation or in some other area of her life. She chooses a conversation partner to tell her story to. An imaginary boundary separates the presenter and partner from the listeners who comprise a reflecting team. Reflecting teams are limited to five or six. If more people are present, they become observers.

The process requires a facilitator who keeps time, maintains the boundary, and helps the group stay focused. He may be a part of the reflecting team.

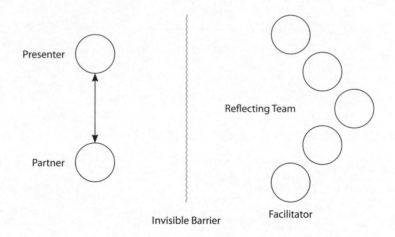

This way of presenting a case places people in an "overhearing" position. First, the reflecting team overhears the conversation between the presenter and her partner. Then the presenter and partner take an overhearing position as reflecting team members talk among themselves about the conversation they have overheard. A key to the power of this way of presenting a case is to maintain the boundary between presenter and partner on the one hand and the reflecting team on the other, so there is no cross talk until the last period of the process. When the boundary is breached, the power of the experience is diminished.

A case presentation takes an hour and follows this sequence:

1. *The presenter tells the listening partner the story of the case* (20 minutes). The presenter speaks to the partner as if no one else is present, telling the story of her encounter with a person or group. The case may or may not be written. We found that problem-saturated cases were not the only ones that provided rich learning material. Without any preparation beforehand, clergy can make an impromptu presentation by selecting a question from several, such as: What recent situation has taught you something important about yourself? What is a recent success, and how did you get there? What person or persons have been the human face of God for you?

   The partner's responsibilities are (1) to listen with curiosity, from time to time asking clarifying questions, and (2) *to ask questions that focus on the inner world of the presenter more than on the person or persons being reported on.*

2. *Silence following the presentation provides a transition* (1 minute). Silence permits the conversation to come to rest, to keep the pace deliberate, and to give the reflecting team time to ponder what they have heard.

3. *The reflecting team members talk among themselves about what they have heard* (14 minutes). The boundary is maintained, and the presenter and partner remain silent. Members of the reflecting team do not speak to the presenter and partner, only to each other.

Guidelines for the Reflecting Team[4]

   a. Team members participate together in a conversation, building on each other's ideas. The total number of ideas is kept small.

   b. Team members don't try to instruct or lead the team. Questions are asked and ideas are offered tentatively, usually in the subjunctive mood.

c. Team members comment only on what has occurred in the preceding conversation and not beyond it.

d. Team members situate their ideas in their own experience. They do not speak as experts but rather out of their personal life and subjectivity.

e. In the overall conversation, team members allow space for every member of the team to have a voice.

f. Team members aim for brevity in their comments.

g. Team members elicit responses from other team members; *they don't operate as a panel, making separate speeches.*

4. *The presenter and partner respond to what they have heard* (10 minutes). The boundary between them and the reflecting team is maintained. The focus of this dialogue is on the reflecting team conversation and how it has affected the presenter. It is easy for the presenter to move away from the reflecting team conversation. *The task of the partner at this stage, therefore, is to help the presenter stay focused on what the reflecting team has said and what may be learned from them.* The partner also pays attention to the presenter's affect and follows these feelings.

5. *The boundary is removed and all speak together* (15 minutes). The removal of the boundary changes the conversation so that all participants can talk as one group about the content and the process of the case presentation. If there are observers beyond the reflecting team, this is an opportunity for them to report their observations.

Conclusion. At the end of the hour, conversation about the case stops, and the group moves on to other matters. There may be an inclination to continue the conversation about the case; however, it is best to keep it within the time boundaries of the case presentation. The case presentation structure is a container that keeps the presenter and group focused and located in a not-knowing, curious place. If the conversation continues beyond the case time, this focus is lost. The presentation experience can be powerful and very full.

Clear closure at the end of the hour allows the presenter and the group to fully disengage. Unclear boundaries can invite casual conversation that diminishes or distracts from the case hour.

Summary of the Case Presentation Agenda

Minutes	Activity
20	The Presenter tells the case to the listening partner.
1	Silence.
14	The members of the reflecting team talk among themselves about what they have overheard, keeping the focus on the presenter.
10	The presenter responds in conversation with the listening partner; the listening partner helps the presenter focus on what has been overheard from the reflecting team.
15	The boundary is removed so that all join in the conversation.

GUIDELINES FOR
CONSTRUCTING GENOGRAMS

A genogram is a family tree that allows persons to see, thicken, and perform their personal narrative. A genogram of clergy persons allows ministers to see how family relationship patterns may be re-played by them in the congregational family. This genogram work occurs in two phases. *The first phase is drawing the genogram.* We recommend doing this work as a group where members can consult with each other and with a facilitator. *The second phase is telling the story of your genogram to your group.* If you draw the genogram on large easel paper, then others will be able to see it in your presenta-tion. You tell your story of your genogram to the group. Group members ask curious questions and wonder with you about aspects of the family story.

The genogram on the following page shows a minister's family with four generations of ministers.

Observations and Questions about the Genogram

The focal person and the one drawing this genogram is Robert Ad-ams, age 43, a Presbyterian minister. He is married to Abby Carr, who is a high school principal, and they have a son, Brad (12), and a daughter, Jennifer (10). Some persons are named in the genogram and some are not, because either Robert does not consider them central to his story or doesn't have information about them.

The emotional lines show that Robert's great-grandfather, Wil-liam Ransom Adams, was an Episcopal minister, as was Robert's grandfather, Todd Vernon Adams. The dotted lines show emotion-al distance between them. Robert's father, William, is a Presbyte-rian minister, and one can see the probable influence of Williams's mother-in-law, Suzan Winters, a Presbyterian minister, on this change in denominational affiliation.

Questions Robert may consider as he makes his presentation or that might be brought up from the group could include: (1) What is the story of the change from emotional distance, seen in the

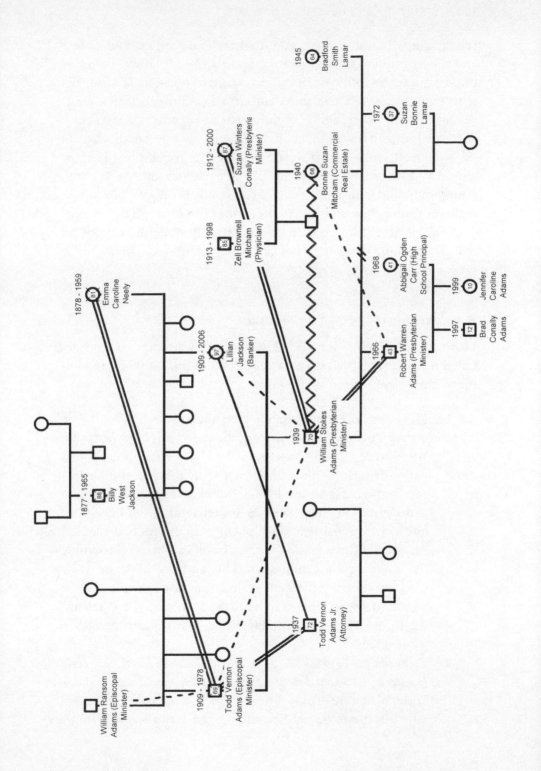

relationships between great grandfather, grandfather, and father, and the emotional closeness between you and your father? (2) How important is the influence of Suzan Winters on your relationship with your father? (3) You show emotional distance between yourself and your mother, and your father shows an emotional distance between him and his mother; what influence do you see this having on your relationships with women in the congregation? (4) How would you describe the influence of your parent's divorce on you, your family, and your ministry? (5) The family is full of male and female professional persons; what effect does this legacy have on you?

Questions of the presenter should strictly obey the rule of no fixing, advising, or saving, and also include *no interpreting*. The presenter is the sole interpreter.

Resources for Preparing Genograms

How do you draw a genogram? Rather than attempt to give detailed instructions about doing a genogram in this book, we recommend these resources:

1. McGoldrick, Monica, Randy Gerson, and Sueli Petry. *Genograms: Assessment and Intervention*. 3rd ed. New York: W. W. Norton, 2008. First published in 1985, this book is written by family therapists for use in therapy and health-care settings. It shows how to draw genograms and how genograms can help families understand the influence of intergenerational relationships on present family dynamics. Any of the three editions of the book can be used to guide the building of genograms. The authors illustrate their work by showing the genograms of famous people such as Sigmund Freud, the Kennedys, Ted Turner, the Clintons, the Roosevelts, Katherine Hepburn, and Princess Diana, to name a few.

2. Richardson, Ronald W. *Family Ties That Bind: A Self-Help Guide to Change through Family of Origin Therapy*. New York: Midpoint Trade Books, 1999. This brief book is a self-help guide for understanding the way the generations

of families shape current family relationships. It provides abbreviated guidelines for doing a genogram.

3. www.genopro.com is a downloadable program for building genograms. One can learn to use it quickly, and it offers a free trial period to allow a test run to see how it works. It provides quick lists of genogram symbols.

4. www.genogram.org is the earliest computerized program for drawing genograms. It does not have a free trial period.

5. www.interpersonaluniverse.net provides its software by mail. You can order free demonstration disks.

Keep It Simple

While these books and programs provide guidance for drawing a genogram, they also tempt one to get lost in the technology of drawing a sophisticated family tree. *Avoid this temptation!* All you need is the basic genogram structure and a few additional symbols to describe emotional relationships. You will also invent your own symbols, which you can explain when you present your genogram. If the genogram looks messy, that's okay. The main job of the genogram is to lay out family relationships over three or four generations in a way that will elicit the family's stories.

Narratives from the Genograms

A genogram can open doors to many stories. The stories emerge in the drawing process as well as in the presentation process. *These narratives are keys to understanding your own story and how it developed.* Among the accounts that turn up in the genogram, you may look for stories about:

1. The family's resilience and strength.
2. Conflicts among family members.
3. Situations of harm or abuse.
4. Family secrets and their power.
5. The family's formal religion (what's formally professed) and its functional religion (the religion that's been lived out).

6. Religious differences.
7. How the family has shaped your ministry—the way you lead and care for others.
8. Unresolved conflicts that have been passed from one generation to the next.
9. Emotional cutoffs where family members avoid each other for long periods.
10. Political or philosophical positions and differences.
11. Appreciation for the absurd and ability to laugh at the family's peculiarities.
12. What is left out of the picture—people, relationships, events.

One Piece of the Puzzle

The genogram is one strategy for understanding your story of yourself. It's one piece of the puzzle. How does it fit with the other strategies—your earliest childhood memory, one of your favorite biblical narratives, an account of your leadership before you were twenty, and your case presentations?

COLLECTING AND ORGANIZING IDEAS FROM A GROUP

A narrative clergy group was trying to decide what topics they wanted to consider during the next six months of meetings. They decided to base these topics on the things they most enjoyed doing in their ministry. The group members used the following process to find out what topics to pursue during the next six meetings.

This procedure can be used to answer many priority questions in a group when the group wants to know, "What do we *as a group* believe to be the most important things in this list of possibilities?"

The Process

1. Participants met in pairs to discuss what they most enjoyed doing in ministry and listed them on paper.
2. Upon convening in the large group, the facilitator went around the table asking for an item from each person. In a couple of rounds all the items were posted on an easel pad.
3. Each item was identified by an alphabetical letter.
4. Duplicate items were eliminated.
5. There were fifteen items (after combining two) and the formula $N/3$ was used to determine the number of choices each person was given. $15/3$ = five items.
6. Participants wrote down their five choices.
7. The facilitator read each item and asked people to raise their hand to vote for their choice. The number of votes was placed to the left of the item.
8. Needing six topics for the upcoming six sessions, the six items with the highest numbers were marked.

The Rules

1. Avoid trying to combine things that seem related, or you'll end up with only one or two items.

2. If a possible duplicate is identified, everyone has to agree or the items remain separate.

3. Doubling up on choices is not permitted (e.g., choosing item A twice).

The Results

1. A final list is ordered by the most to the least votes.
2. All the original items are included.
3. The top six are separated from the rest.

Votes	Item
	THE TOP SIX
4	Teaching—the challenge of give and take in the teaching moment
4	Research for preaching and writing
3	Using the power of questions to open up thinking
3	Rolling up our sleeves to do mission work—organizing; seeing the transformation of laity who do the mission work
3	Handling the gift of power earned in the congregation
3	Discipleship work—the joy of seeing people "get it"
	THE OTHERS
2	Leading—helping people come to consensus
2	Pastoral care situations—no agenda; representing faith
2	Ministry to people in life stages—working in these liminal moments
1	Mentoring other rabbis and clergy professionals
1	Thickening the music program
1	Working with youth—teaching confirmation classes
1	The freedom of ministry—not having to punch a clock
0	Being a member of the choir, a group where I as pastor am not the leader
0	Worship Planning

The Use of the List

The group leaders shared the results with the group. They used the list to guide the creation of topics for the following meetings. The items didn't give the exact topics but provided the clues needed to follow the group's collective wisdom for shaping the themes for the next six months.

CLOSING A MEETING
WITH TIME TO REFLECT

1. A meeting is a story of a group of people gathered for some purpose. Stories need a conclusion. Reflecting on the meeting is a way to provide a conclusion to the story.

2. Reflecting on a meeting also helps people distinguish between content (the *what* of the meeting) and process (the *how* of the meeting). Most meetings focus exclusively on the *what*, the content of the meeting, and give no attention to *how* people are doing what they do in the meeting.

   a. It may be difficult for a group to distinguish between content and process. Use examples: "Joanne proposed we postpone the next meeting for a month. That's the *what*, the content. The way she did it was to ask a question, 'Do you think we will be ready to take action at next month's meeting?' That's the *how*, the process. She could have said, 'We have to postpone our next meeting.' What's different about that *how*, that process?"

   b. Paying attention to process (*how*) can occur during the meeting and not just at the end. Sam said, "I'm getting anxious about our making a final decision when I hear several different views on this. I'd like us to take a straw vote to see where we stand right now. What do you think?"

3. Reflecting on process at the end of a meeting can bring a sense of satisfaction and accomplishment to the group. "An hour ago I thought for sure we were bogged down for the rest of the meeting," Andrea said, "and then Marilyn came up with a different way to look at the problem. That got us unstuck. After that we were able to move quickly to a plan. And we're ending on time."

4. A conversation about the process of the meeting allows people to say what they believe worked well and what

they believe needs to be changed for future meetings. You can focus on this perspective on the meeting by using a flip chart:

+	▲
The plus sign represents the positive things people express about the process of the meeting; list these here.	The triangle represents the Greek letter delta, which is a sign for change; list on this side the changes people want to see.

5. Reflecting at the end of a meeting is a hopeful activity that says:

   a. Those in charge of the meeting *care* about how well or how poorly the meeting goes.
   b. If the meeting is not going well for members, they can alter future meetings by making recommendations for change.

6. Taking time to reflect on a meeting or inviting people to make process observations during the meeting helps distribute the power in the meeting toward partnerships rather than toward top-down leadership.

Notes

Introduction

1. In 1990 Michael White in Australia and David Epston in New Zealand published the first book on narrative therapy, *Narrative Means to Therapeutic Ends* (New York: W. W. Norton & Co.). In 2007, after almost two decades of narrative practice, White published his definitive work *Maps of Narrative Practice* (New York: W. W. Norton & Co.), a year before his untimely death on April 4, 2008.

Chapter One

1. Adler, 73–74.
2. See Crossan, *The Historial Jesus*, 43–46, who draws upon the theory of Gerhard Lenski.
3. Funk, 327.
4. See Herzog, 194–214.
5. See Dozier, *The Dream of God*.

Chapter Two

1. Bass, *The Practicing Congregation*, 99–100.
2. Bass, "Living the Story."
3. Turner, *The Ritual Process*, 95–96.
4. Genesis 18:1–15.
5. Palmer, 114.

6. Hester, "Early Memory and Narrative Therapy," 339.
7. Ibid., 344–345.
8. For an interpretation of the overhearing principle in preaching, see Craddock, *Overhearing the Gospel.*
9. Ibid., 103–20.
10. Solman, "An American Classic."
11. The idea of a "reflecting team" grew out of family therapy as it was influenced by narrative thought; see Tom Andersen, ed., *The Reflecting Team.*
12. Based on a theory of James Paul Gee, *An Introduction to Discourse Analysis,* chapters 5–7.

Chapter Three

1. Borg, *Meeting Jesus Again for the First Time.*
2. Ibid., 75–79.
3. Matthew 7:13–14.
4. Borg, *Meeting Jesus,* 80–85.
5. Borg, *Jesus: Uncovering the Life, Teachings, and Relevance of a Religious Revolutionary,* 217.
6. Palmer, *A Hidden Wholeness,* 58–59.
7. Ibid., 76.
8. This understanding of not-knowing is drawn from Harlene Anderson, *Conversation, Language, and Possibilities,* 134–56.
9. Lincoln, "Second Inaugural Address," 555.
10. Mark 10:42–45, The New Jerusalem Bible.

Chapter Four

1. Alexander, *Victor Turner Revisited,* 27–44.
2. Ibid., 40.
3. The participant did not write this as a poem, but his prose had a poetic rhythm, and we put it into a poem without changing any words.
4. Luke 14:21.

5. Crossan, *Jesus: A Revolutionary Biography*, 68.
6. Ibid.
7. Wellhausen, 71.
8. Ibid., 77.
9. Exodus 20:2–3.
10. Brueggemann, *Covenanted Self*, 25–27. Brueggemann credits Gottwald, 93–99, for an interpretation of the egalitarian social structure that grew out of the Sinai covenant.
11. David Verner of our project staff coined the term "assumptive covenants."
12. For a full interpretation of Bowen family systems theory, see Kerr and Bowen.
13. Friedman, 229.
14. Luke 4:16–21.
15. Freire, 118. For a use of Freire's theory to understand Jesus's parables, see Herzog.
16. Psalm 139:13–14.
17. Exodus 20:11.
18. Deuteronomy 5:15.
19. Brueggemann, *Theology of the Old Testament*, 185.
20. Muller, 77–79.
21. Exodus 20:2–3.
22. Exodus 18:13–24 provides the full account of Moses's encounter with Jethro.
23. Kaner, 278–81.
24. Exodus 15:20.
25. 2 Samuel 6:14.
26. Friedman, 50–51.

Chapter Five

1. Matthew 11:19.
2. Carse, 3.
3. Ibid., 12–24.
4. Ibid., 12, 19.
5. Robinson, 12.

6. Heifetz, 73–76.
7. Robinson, 19–20.
8. Bass, *The Practicing Congregation*, 99–100.
9. Bass, "Living the Story."

Chapter Six

1. Triangle Pastoral Counseling, the home of this clergy project, has adopted the narrative case model with a reflecting team as the format for its weekly case conferences. This model replaced an earlier format in which a psychiatrist led the case conference. The influence of the narrative case model has radiated out into the rest of the organization, strengthening the sense of community and equality among staff members.
2. Luke 7:33–34.
3. The idea of "ordaining moments" is from Logan C. Jones.
4. Alexander, "Pentecostal Possession and Grotowski's Ritual Projects as Social Protest," 21, italics added. The quote is Alexander's version of Turner's several definitions.
5. Carson, 101–102.
6. See Kay's poem that she carved out of the text of her interview on page 39.
7. Monk et al., eds., 3.
8. John Wimmer, letter to the authors, November 21, 2008.
9. Bass, *Christianity for the Rest of Us*, 193. Bass uses the gap metaphor to describe people in mainline Protestant churches who "had rediscovered the humility of spiritual liberality." She says liberality is "that genuine openness which reminds us that in the economy of the universe, we are only human and, despite our marvelous intellectual capabilities, there will always be things we cannot know. In that gap God breathes, and there, we experience awe."

Conclusion

1. Borg, *Meeting Jesus Again for the First Time.*

Resources

1. See Intrator and Scribner, *Leading from Within*, an excellent source of poems for narrative groups.
2. Bass, *The Practicing Congregation*, 99–100.
3. Bass, "Living the Story."
4. Based on Freedman and Combs, chapter 7.

Bibliography

Adler, Alfred. *What Life Should Mean to You*. Boston: Little, Brown and Co., 1931.

Alexander, Bobby C. "Pentecostal Possession and Grotowski's Ritual Projects as Social Protest: A Critical Assessment of Victor Turner's Theory of 'Ritual Anti-structure' as an Interpretive Tool." PhD diss., Columbia University, 1985.

————. *Victor Turner Revisited: Ritual as Social Change*. Atlanta: Scholars Press, 1991.

Andersen, Tom, ed. *The Reflecting Team: Dialogues and Dialogues about the Dialogues*. New York: W. W. Norton & Co., 1991.

Anderson, Harlene. *Conversation, Language, and Possibilities: A Postmodern Approach to Therapy*. New York: Basic Books, 1997.

Bass, Diana Butler. *Christianity for the Rest of Us: How the Neighborhood Church Is Transforming the Faith*. New York: HarperCollins, 2006.

————. "Living the Story." *Alban Weekly*, January 22, 2007, http://www.alban.org/conversation.aspx?id=3386

————. *The Practicing Congregation: Imagining a New Old Church*. Herndon, VA: Alban Publications, 2004.

Borg, Marcus J. *Jesus: Uncovering the Life, Teachings, and Relevance of a Religious Revolutionary*. San Francisco: HarperSanFrancisco, 2006.

————. *Meeting Jesus Again for the First Time: The Historical Jesus and the Heart of Contemporary Faith*. San Francisco: HarperSanFrancisco, 1994.

Brueggemann, Walter. *The Covenanted Self: Explorations in Law and Covenant*. Minneapolis: Augsburg Fortress, 1999.

———. *Theology of the Old Testament: Testimony, Dispute, Advocacy*. Minneapolis: Fortress Press, 1997.

Carse, James P. *The Religious Case against Belief*. New York: Penguin Press, 2008.

Carson, Timothy L. *Liminal Reality and Transformational Power*. Lanham, NY: University Press of America, 1997.

Craddock, Fred B. *Overhearing the Gospel*. Revised and expanded ed. St. Louis, MO: Chalice Press, 2002.

Crossan, John Dominic. *The Historical Jesus: The Life of a Mediterranean Jewish Peasant*. San Francisco: HarperSanFrancisco, 1991.

———. *Jesus: A Revolutionary Biography*. San Fransisco: HarperSanFransisco, 1994.

Dozier, Verna J. *The Dream of God: A Call to Return*. Boston: Cowley Publications, 1991.

Freedman, Jill, and Gene Combs. *Narrative Therapy: The Social Construction of Preferred Realities*. New York: W. W. Norton & Co., 1996.

Freire, Paulo. *Pedagogy of the Oppressed*. Translated by Myra Bergman Ramos. 30th anniversary ed. New York: Continuum, 2002.

Friedman, Edwin H. *Generation to Generation: Family Process in Church and Synagogue*. New York: Guilford Press, 1985.

Funk, Robert W. *The Five Gospels: What Did Jesus Really Say? The Search for the Authentic Words of Jesus*. San Francisco: HarperSanFrancisco, 1993.

Gee, James Paul. *An Introduction to Discourse Analysis: Theory and Method*. London: Routledge, 1999.

Gottwald, Norman K. *The Tribes of Yahweh: A Sociology of the Religion of Liberated Israel, 1250–1050 B.C.* Maryknoll: Orbis Books, 1979.

Heifetz, Ronald. *Leadership without Easy Answers*. Cambridge, MA: Harvard University Press, 1994.

Herzog, William. *Parables as Subversive Speech: Jesus as Pedagogue of the Oppressed*. Louisville: Westminster/John Knox, 1994.

Hester, Richard L. "Early Memory and Narrative Therapy." *The Journal of Individual Psychology* 60, no. 4 (2004): 338–47.

Intrator, Sam, and Megan Scribner. *Leading from Within: Poetry That Sustains the Courage to Lead*. San Francisco: Jossey-Bass, 2007.

Kaner, Sam. *Facilitator's Guide to Participatory Decision-Making*. 2nd ed. San Francisco: Jossey-Bass, 2007.

Kerr, Michael E., and Murray Bowen. *Family Evaluation: An Approach Based on Bowen Theory*. New York: W. W. Norton & Co., 1988.

Lenski, Gerhard. *Power and Privilege: A Theory of Social Stratification*. New York: McGraw-Hill, 1966.

Lincoln, Abraham. "Second Inaugural Address." In *The Annals of America*. Vol. 18. Edited by Mortimer J. Adler. Chicago: Encyclopaedia Britannica, Inc., 1968.

McGoldrick, Monica, Randy Gerson, and Sueli Petry. *Genograms: Assessment and Intervention*. 3rd ed. New York: W. W. Norton & Co., 2008.

Monk, Gerald, John Winslade, Kathie Crocket, and David Epston, eds. *Narrative Therapy in Practice: The Archaeology of Hope*. San Francisco: Jossey-Bass, 1997.

Muller, Wayne. *Sabbath: Finding Rest, Renewal, and Delight in Our Busy Lives*. New York: Bantam Books, 1999.

Palmer, Parker J. *A Hidden Wholeness*. San Francisco: Jossey-Bass, 2004.

Richardson, Ronald W. *Family Ties That Bind: A Self-Help Guide to Change through Family of Origin Therapy*. New York: Midpoint Trade Books, 1999.

Robinson, Anthony. *Transforming Congregational Culture*. Grand Rapids, MI: Eerdmans Publishing, 2003.

Solman, Paul. "An American Classic." MacNeil/Lehrer Productions. February 10, 1999. Online at www.pbs.org.

Turner, Victor. *The Ritual Process: Structure and Anti-Structure*. New York: Aldine De Gruyter, 1995.

Wellhausen, Julius. *Prolegomena to the History of Ancient Israel*. Cleveland and New York: The World Publishing Company, 1957.

White, Michael. *Maps of Narrative Practice*. New York: W. W. Norton & Co., 2007.

White, Michael, and David Epston. *Narrative Means to Therapeutic Ends*. New York: W. W. Norton & Co., 1990.